Paul  ch

All About the Months

ALL ABOUT THE
MONTHS

MAYMIE R. KRYTHE

 HARPER & ROW, PUBLISHERS

NEW YORK AND LONDON

The publisher wishes to thank The Macmillan Company for permission to re-print selections from *September Day* appearing in DARK OF THE MOON by Sara Teasdale, Copyright 1926, The Macmillan Company, Copyright renewed 1954 by Mamie T. Wheless; and from *Last Chrysanthemum* appearing in COLLECTED POEMS OF THOMAS HARDY by Thomas Hardy, Copyright 1925, The Macmillan Company.

LIBRARY OF CONGRESS CATALOG CARD NUMBER: 66–18584

M-Q

To Martha Elteen Kirschbaum

Contents

Foreword

According to authorities, a calendar (from *Kalends*, or *Calends*) is a system of reckoning time—an orderly arrangement of the divisions of the days, weeks, months, and years adapted to civil life.

From the earliest days man has evolved varied systems of measuring time, with calculations involving the sun, moon, stars, and tides. During the seventh century B.C. Numa Pompilius revised a primitive Roman calendar containing ten months, and added the two months of *Januarius* and *Februarius*. Then in 46 B.C. Julius Caesar reformed this calendar, adopted the Egyptian solar year, and established one of 365¼ days. No further changes were made until 1582, when Pope Gregory XIII had eleven days dropped and a new system of leap years worked out. Allowing for the difference between the Julian year and the astronomical year, he came up with 365 days, or 366 during leap years.

Today the Gregorian calendar is still in use, although the Julian calendar is sometimes referred to for reckoning certain religious festivals.

Birthstones and Flowers of the Month

For centuries it has been customary to wear jewels and use flowers that are symbolic of the month of one's birth, and following are those given as in favor today:

	Birthstone	Flower
JANUARY:	garnet	carnation or snowdrop
FEBRUARY:	amethyst	violet or primrose
MARCH:	bloodstone or aquamarine	jonquil or daffodil
APRIL:	diamond	sweet pea or daisy
MAY:	emerald	lily of the valley or hawthorn
JUNE:	pearl, moonstone or alexandrite	rose or honeysuckle
JULY:	ruby	larkspur or water lily
AUGUST:	sardonyx or peridot	poppy or gladiolus
SEPTEMBER:	sapphire	aster or morning glory
OCTOBER:	opal or tourmaline	calendula or cosmos
NOVEMBER:	topaz	chrysanthemum
DECEMBER:	turquoise or zircon	narcissus or holly

January

... in came old January, wrapped well
In many weeds to keep the cold away.
—EDMUND SPENSER

JANUARY, the first and coldest month of the year received its
name from the Latin, "Januarius" (derived from *janua*, meaning
door). The word came from the name of the Roman deity, Janus,
to whom the Romans' first month was sacred. It looked both to the
past and to the future, and was consecrated by offerings of new
products such as wine, salt, meal, and frankincense.

On New Year's Day, the Romans exchanged gifts of small coins;
on one side of them was Janus, the two-faced god, and on the other
a ship, for he was considered the protector of ships and trade.

Janus, according to one source, was an old king of Latium, whose
worship had been introduced by Romulus. In January the Feast of
Agonia was celebrated in his honor, at his citadel on the Janiculum
Hill. Its double gate was kept closed while the land was at peace, but
remained open in time of war. During the Christian era, this portal
is said to have been closed only four times.

The beginnings of each day, month, and year were sacred to
Janus. Preceding any important undertaking, he was invoked before any other deity. The Romans believed that at dawn Janus
opened the gates of heaven to let out the morning, and that he

closed them at dusk. Therefore, he was worshiped as the god of all doors, gates, and entrances, and under his protection too were "the beginnings of all human enterprises."

Several ancient poets sang praises of Janus and his powers:

> 'Tis he! the two-faced Janus comes in view . . .
> But smiles upon the new
> Emerging year with pride;
> And now unlocks with agate key
> The ruby gates of orient day . . .
>   —WILLIAM HONE

> Hark, the cock crows, and yon bright star
> Tells us the day himself's not far . . .
> With him oft Janus doth appear,
> Peeping into the future year.

Janus, as the porter or doorkeeper, was shown with a staff in one hand denoting his power, while a key in the other symbolized his right to open and close all things. Sometimes the god held the number "CCC" (300) in his right hand, and "LXV" (65) in his left, to represent the number of days in the year.

On early coins Janus was depicted with two bearded faces, looking in opposite directions; for there was a belief that he knew both past and future happenings. This was also emblematic of the fact that doors open in two directions. At the time of Emperor Hadrian, this deity was pictured with four faces, in a temple of four sides, with three windows in each. This temple represented the four seasons, and the windows the twelve months over which Janus presided.

The Saxons termed the first month of the year "Wulf-monath," or "Wolf monat, or month," because at this season starving wolves often invaded their villages and attacked human beings. For the lower animals, on which the wolves had been accustomed to feed, had perished during the inclement weather; therefore the wolves had to seek food outside the forests.

Another Saxon name for January was "Aefter-Yula" or "After-Christmas." On some early calendars and church service books, the month of January was shown as a woodsman, carrying an ax, gathering fagots, and blowing on his hands because of the bitter cold.

> Stern winter congeals every brook,
> That murmured so lately with glee
> And places a snowy peruke
> On the head of each bald-pated tree.
> —WILLIAM HONE

In *The Shepherd's Calendar*, the poet, John Clare (1793–1864), pictures an English farmer during the month of January:

> Now musing o'er the changing scene,
> Farmers behind the tavern screen
> Collect; with elbow idly press'd
> On hob, reclines the corner's guest,
> Reading the news to mark again
> The bankrupt list, or price of grain,
> Puffing the while his red-tipt pipe,
> He dreams o'er troubles nearly ripe;
> Yet winter's leisure to regale,
> Hopes better times and sips his ale.

January is the birth-month of many noted individuals, including three of our Chief Executives: Millard Fillmore, William McKinley, and Franklin D. Roosevelt. Other celebrities born the first month of the year are Paul Revere, General Tom Thumb, George Washington Carver, Lord Byron, Carl Sandburg, Ethan Allen, Jack London, Sir Francis Drake, Lloyd George, Wolfgang Amadeus Mozart, Daniel Webster, and Edgar Allan Poe.

The following also observed their birthdays in January: Benjamin Franklin, Robert E. Lee, Stonewall Jackson, Sir Isaac Newton, Alexander Hamilton, Edmund Burke, Francis Bacon, Frederick the Great, Robert Burns, Franz Schubert, and Anna Pavlova. Albert Schweitzer and Benedict Arnold both arrived on January 14.

Various notable events, too, have occurred during the first month:

In 1265 the first English Parliament met; in 1649 Charles I was beheaded; in 1778 France recognized the independence of the American Colonies; in 1784 the peace treaty between Great Britain and the United States was ratified; in 1789 our first national election resulted in the choice of George Washington as President; in 1815 the Battle of New Orleans was fought; in 1802 the Library of Congress had its first librarian; in 1803 The Louisiana Purchase took place; in 1840 penny postage was established; in 1848 gold was discovered in California; in 1863 the Emancipation Proclamation was issued; and in 1883 the Civil Service Act was passed.

In 1902 the first football game in the Rose Bowl was played; in 1903 the treaty with Panama was signed; in 1912 Captain Robert Scott reached the South Pole; in 1913 parcel post was established; in 1915 New York and San Francisco were united by telephone; in 1925 the first woman Governor in the United States was elected in Wyoming; in 1927 the first telephone message traveled across the Atlantic; in 1932 a woman was elected to the U.S. Senate for the first time; in 1946 the United Nations opened its first Assembly; in 1948 Mohandas Gandhi, Indian political leader, was assassinated; in 1954 the U.S. launched its first atomic submarine; in 1957 our first satellite (Explorer I) was in orbit; and in 1959 Fidel Castro took over in Cuba.

January has some important holidays, with the New Year's Day celebration a highlight. This date has long been a time for reflection and resolution. Many are eager to get rid of the old and take on the new.

Once someone declared: "So the first month of the year, like its namesake, looks back over the past, and forward to the future, with hope and good resolutions."

And Alfred Tennyson, in his famous lines, has well expressed this feeling:

> Ring out, wild bells, to the wild, wild sky . . .
> The year is dying in the night . . .
> Ring out, wild bells, and let him die.
> Ring out the old, ring in the new . . .
> Ring out the false, ring in the true.

The evening of January 5 is Twelfth Night, the end of Christmas festivities. Epiphany, celebrated on January 6 (Twelfth-Tide or Old Christmas) commemorates Christ's baptism; it is also the Feast Day of the Three Kings, in remembrance of their visit to Bethlehem.

Another important day to Americans comes just once in four years on January 20, after the Presidential election of the preceding November. This is Inauguration Day; it was set by the 20th Amendment to the Constitution and was ratified by the states in 1933. It is a legal holiday only in Washington, D.C. Franklin Delano Roosevelt was the first U.S. President to take office on this date, instead of the former March 4.

January Birthstone—Garnet

The garnet is hard, durable, and translucent; therefore it makes a beautiful gem stone. However, some are too soft for ring settings, while others are hard enough for use as abrasives.

The word "garnet" originated from a Latin term, *granatus*, meaning "seed-like," for the garnet crystals, embedded in the matrix, resembled pomegranate seeds. Also, red, the most common color of garnets, looked like the thick juice of this fruit.

The gem has been known from time immemorial, and was used, not only for ornamentation, but for smelting ores and polishing various surfaces. The garnet is considered a semi-precious stone. Since it has been found practically in all parts of the world, in different kinds of rocks, and in great abundance, this stone has not been too highly prized for jewelry, and because it is one of the cheapest of gems, its extraction has not been too profitable.

People usually think of the garnet only as a stone of a dark red shade. But its color varies with its composition; besides ruby red and deep red, other hues are yellow, brownish-green, yellow-green, green, purple, and even black. The garnet of greatest value to the jewelry trade is the deep-red variety, the "pyrope," from a Greek word denoting "fire-like."

Garnets differ, too, in size, varying from small ones to exceptionally large specimens. For example, in the Imperial Treasury in Vienna, there was one the size of a pigeon's egg. Kaiser Rudolf II owned a large garnet, valued at 7,000 pounds (about $20,000 in American money). The King of Saxony had such a gem, weighing 468½ carats, set in the Order of the Golden Fleece. And in 1885, a garnet, nine pounds in weight, was found just off Broadway, in New York, by some workmen during an excavating job.

Some garnets are quite brittle and are not easily engraved, and it is remarkable that ancient engravers were able to carve them so skillfully and artistically. In the Marlborough collection, there is a beautiful and famous Roman intaglio, "The Head of the Dog, Sirius." Another unusual garnet has on it the heads of Plato and Socrates. It is asserted that, by means of this engraved stone, it has been possible to identify the likenesses of the two great philosophers.

In using garnets for jewelry, various superstitions have been built up around them. People born in January were supposed to have worn these gems as protection against sickness. This belief is said to have started in Poland, and from there spread to other places on the continent and then abroad.

It was thought, also, that a garnet could protect its owner from accidents when traveling; that it had certain qualities connected with blood, and could impart to those whose birthdays were during January such magical characteristics as "constancy," "true fellowship," and "fidelity." In addition, anyone who wore a garnet with a lion engraved upon it would be blessed with health and honor. Sometimes these stones were crushed and used in poultices to stimulate the heart.

According to an ancient legend in the Talmud, the only light Noah had in his famous Ark came from an enormous red garnet. Pliny, the well-known Latin writer, stated that large garnets, or carbuncles, were sometimes hollowed out and used as drinking vessels. In 1791, the French crown jewels collection contained eight cups, each made from a large, single garnet.

In primitive days, some Asiatic peoples used these stones as bullets, for they believed the glowing shade of the gems made them more deadly. The Persians considered garnets as royal stones, and often engraved the likeness of their monarchs on them.

While garnets are found in varied parts of the globe, certain places have supplied the majority of them. South Africa, for instance, has been a good source for these gems. In 1870, a Dutch overseer named de Klerk found garnets on a farm in Orange Colony. At once he suspected the presence of diamonds, as these two stones are often found close together; and de Klerk was right.

Numerous deep-red garnets have been mined in South Africa; however, they did not sell well until re-named "Cape rubies." Another kind, varying from golden-yellow to cinnamon-brown, has been exploited as "Transvaal jade," but in reality it has no connection with jade.

India and Burma produce dark crimson or violet-red stones named "almandine" or "carbuncle." The latter means "a little spark," and is often cut in hollow cabochon form.

Quantities of attractive orange-colored garnets come from southwestern Ceylon. Ratnapur, "city of gems," is the center of this industry. Natives carry soil containing the stones to a nearby stream, where they pick them out by hand. A cinnamon-colored garnet also is found in Ceylon; and this same type has been discovered in the lava of Mt. Vesuvius.

In the latter part of the 1800's, some handsome and quite brilliant olive-green garnets were found in Russia, on the European side of the Ural Mountains. At first, these green varieties were mistaken for emeralds and were termed "Uralian emeralds." Later they proved to be garnets of the andradite type, with unusual transparency. On the market, these sell for the highest price per carat of any of the garnet family. They look well in pendants and necklaces, but are not hard enough for use in finger rings.

There was just one place in the world where garnets were found in such abundance as to warrant their collection and preparation. This was Teplitz, in Czechoslovakia, about fifty miles from Prague. They were dark red, and became well known as "Bohemian garnets."

The garnet industry was carried on at Teplitz for centuries, and as many as 10,000 persons were engaged in cutting and setting the gems. Their good red color made them suitable for peasant jewelry, and countless pieces were purchased by visitors to the region.

However, in the latter part of the eighteenth century, numerous yellowish-red garnets were taken from the old Bohemian mines. They were mounted in what many people considered unattractive and inartistic pins and brooches with the result that industry and stones lost popularity with those individuals who had "a nice taste in gem stones." Recently, in several places, there have been attempts to revive interest in garnets by giving them such misleading names as "Cape rubies" or "Arizona rubies," and experts declare that these practices should be discouraged.

In the United States, garnets have been discovered in Virginia, Montana, Southern Colorado, and New Mexico. And on Navajo Indian reservations in Arizona and New Mexico natives collect garnets that have been rounded by the scouring of desert sands. Traders and tourists buy these gems set in jewelry by the Indians. North Carolina—Macon County in particular—produces attractive, light violet-colored red garnets, while others from this same state are pale red stones of unusual brilliance.

Although garnets are still fashioned for ornamental purposes, much of the output is now used in other ways, especially as jewels in watches or for bearings in scientific instruments. The common variety is applied to the cutting and polishing of other gems.

About 4,000 tons are made annually into abrasive especially needed by the shoe industry. This product is manufactured from the chips from ordinary garnets cut in Bohemia or Madagascar.

In the United States, New York leads in this industry. There is much high-grade garnet-bearing rock in the Adirondacks; and it is also to be found in New Hampshire, North Carolina, Delaware, Chester County, Pennsylvania, and other places.

At the large New York quarries good mechanical equipment has replaced slower and more expensive methods of extracting the stone. The powdered garnets are used for grinding and polishing plate glass, wood, and leather. "Garnet paper," considered superior to regular sandpaper, is an important commercial product.

If the garnet is your birthstone, remember, it is of value not only for its ornamental qualities, but also for its utility.

January Flower—Carnation

> Carnations and my first love! And he was seventeen
> And I was only twelve—a stately gulf between.
> —MARGARET WIDDEMER

The carnation, dedicated to January, has been a favorite garden flower for many generations, highly valued for its scent and beauty.

Many years ago, William Corbett, an enthusiastic flower lover, declared that he preferred "the plant of a fine carnation to a gold watch set with diamonds." Because of their distinctive fragrance early peoples enjoyed adorning themselves with crowns and garlands of carnations. The flower is still a great favorite in lands bordering on the Mediterranean.

This lovely bloom, "a perennial herb of the pink family, bearing spicy scented flowers with fringed petals," got its name from the primitive variety. It was pink, or flesh-colored. The word, "carnation," was derived from the Latin term, "carnis," meaning "flesh." The Greeks called this plant "dianthus," or "divine flower," for its delicious odor. Few blossoms in the world are so fragrant and spicy as these. However, they were not used so much in early times for perfume as one might suppose.

Some sources say the carnation has been cultivated for more than 2,000 years; that the original grew wild in the Mediterranean countries; that the Greeks raised it before 300 B.C. Pliny wrote that the "clove pink" (a name given by some botanists to the single varieties only) was found in Spain at the time of Augustus Caesar. There the natives used it to give a spicy flavor to beverages. Another historian states that Moslems cultivated carnations in Tunis and took them to Spain during the thirteenth century.

The story goes that "pinks" practically disappeared from the scene for several centuries, then regained popularity during the Renaissance making the carnation the symbol of the high point which civilization had reached. These plants were "supremely the flowers of the Renaissance."

The carnation, or "pink" may have been introduced into the British Isles at the time of the Norman Conquest; also some believe it was taken there by knights returning from the Crusades. Originally it was termed the "gillyflower"; and we often find references to it in English literature.

In his works, Shakespeare mentions carnations:

> The fairest flowers o' the season
> Are our carnations, and streaked gillyvors . . .

Artists often included them in their portraits and interiors. By the middle of the sixteenth century, these plants had been greatly improved in England. William Turner declared, "They have been made pleasant and sweet by the art of man, and not by nature." Gerard wrote in 1597 that pinks were "prominent in gardens and passionately cultivated."

These blooms were sometimes called "sops-in-wine," as they were added to wine, as well as to beer and ale for flavor. Spenser once wrote that young people went out to the woods and brought back

> . . . hawthorn buds and sweet eglantine
> And garlands of roses and sops-in-wine.

In medieval days cooks used "pinks" as food seasoning; sometimes they made conserves, or candied them. These tidbits, as one writer declared, "wonderfully above measure do comfort the heart." The flowers at times were made into a sauce for lamb or mutton, while "tansie" was "a sort of sweet omelet colored with pinks."

Several superstitions became connected with carnations. It was believed that the flower could preserve the human body and also keep away unpleasant dreams. Some persons asserted that "pinks" sprang from the graves of lovers; so the blossoms were popular as funeral wreaths. There was a legend that the carnation was first seen on earth at the time of Christ's birth; therefore it was called "a flower of rejoicing."

Carnations, too, played a role in the history of early medicine. Distilled water—"the perfume made from gillyflowers"—was considered an excellent cure for the "falling sickness." When a person was afflicted by that "baffling ailment" known as "melancholy," carnations were used in preparing drinks for him. One such concoction was named "Lady Button's Melancholy Waters."

Elizabeth Grey, the Countess of Kent, and Hannah Wooley were two Englishwomen who used carnations in their recipes for food they prepared and also in medicines they concocted. Mrs. Wooley, the wife of a schoolmaster, "doctored the pupils without help of any physician."

In the coat of arms of an Italian family of Ronsecco there was a carnation. The story is that Countess Margharita Ronsecco on the eve of her wedding gave her lover a carnation to take with him to the Holy Land where he was going on the crusade to rescue the tomb of Christ from the Saracens. Some time later, a soldier brought her the news that Orlando had been killed in battle. The messenger gave the Countess the withered flower, which her lover's blood had changed from white to red. She planted it as a memorial to her lover, and from it grew a white carnation with a red center.

In England, during the eighteenth century, when these flowers grew out of doors from June to August, various new kinds were developed with such names as "The Fair Maid of Kent," and "Ruffling Robin." The "Anne Boleyn" originated in 1836, and is still grown. Towards the end of the last century carnations "went indoors" in Britain, and were raised extensively in greenhouses. They were the favorite flowers of Sarah, Duchess of Marlborough.

During the last two centuries, the Dutch originated several types of carnations. The French were the first to discover a kind that would flower at times other than the normal season—the "perpetual bloomer." This has also been popular in the United States.

In the early part of the nineteenth century there was a fad taken up by some English gardeners of growing what was called "florists' flowers." These included about eight distinctive varieties, and the growers cultivated them carefully and brought them to perfection. Among those cherished plants were "laced pinks" and carnations.

In 1897 the carnation named "Mrs. W. T. Lawson" received an award from the Royal Horticultural Society. Other improved varieties include "Betsy," "Melrose," "Woburn," "Puritan," and "Barbara Brigham."

Years of efforts by American growers have also resulted in the production of hundreds of kinds of carnations in varied hues ranging from pink to deep crimson. Some have solid colors, others are bi-colored; several have plain petals; others are fringed; however, most blossoms are of the double variety.

In Hawaii, beautiful garlands, or leis, of lovely fragrant carnations are worn both by the flower-loving people of these Pacific Islands and by many visitors.

Today cut carnations are especially popular for indoor decorations as they hold up well. Great quantities are grown under glass, and this has become big business. White carnations worn as boutonnieres have become the distinguishing insignia of ushers at church and at weddings.

On Mother's Day, the second Sunday in May, a white carnation is worn in memory of a deceased mother; the red is worn in honor of that living parent. The flower was chosen for this special occasion as it was the favorite bloom of the mother of Anna Jarvis, who promoted the observance of this holiday.

The carnation was also the favorite of President William McKinley, and he always wore one in his coat lapel. After his death in 1901, Lewis G. Reynolds of Dayton, Ohio, wrote to *The New York Herald Tribune* suggesting that on President McKinley's birthday (January 29) each person wear a carnation in his memory. He declared this would not only "serve the purpose of a perennial memorial to a faithful public servant," but would also foster the spirit of patriotism.

Mr. Reynolds's idea was adopted and a "Carnation Day" observed on January 29 was continued for some time, both in President

McKinley's native state of Ohio and elsewhere. One source stated that such a day is still observed by some Masonic groups. In addition, a "Carnation League" was founded to arouse party interest in political activities.

Alternate January Flower—The Snowdrop

The snowdrop is the alternate flower for January. It is a bulbous European herb, bearing nodding white flowers and belongs to the amaryllis family. The plant produces two leaves, usually a single swan-like bloom, although some have double flowers.

There are ten species of these spring blossoms found around the Mediterranean and in Western Asia. This "flower of character," whose blooms are the first harbingers of spring, is seen in Europe from France to the Caucasus Mountains. The snowdrop is said to have been growing on Mount Hymettus in Greece, in 300 B.C. In 1615 a Hollander stated that it was common in Italy (where monks are said to have introduced it during the fifteenth century); and that snowdrops were not grown in Holland, except "in the gardens of the curious."

The plant is probably not indigenous to the British Isles, however, some botanists, including Sir Thomas Edward Smith, believed it was native to England. Before 1864 Crito wrote:

I can trace most of the wild specimens to some neighboring garden, or old dilapidated monastery; and I am persuaded it was introduced into England by the monks, subsequent to the Conquest, and probably since the time of Chaucer.

Neither Shakespeare nor Chaucer mentioned the snowdrop, and it is the opinion of several authorities that it reached England in the nineteenth century. There it was given such names as "The Fair Maid of February," "Mary's Taper," and "Candlemas Bell." Other names applied to it in different lands include "Virgin Flower," "Snow Piercer," "Winter Gallant," "Little Snow Bell," "Baby Bell," and "Spring Brightness."

The snowdrop is the earliest blooming plant, and often pushes its delicate white bells up through the snow. One source declares that its flowers evolve "as if by the most determined periodical laws." Some say it may have been left behind by glacial ice. The snowdrop is noted as the only plant that can bloom outside in winter. Some years ago, in Cleveland, Ohio, on January 21, such flowers were seen in bloom; and this happened again, three years later. However, the usual flowering period in northern climates is in March or April.

In primitive times the root of the snowdrop was sometimes used as food, also as a dressing for cuts and wounds. These plants were frequently cultivated in monastery gardens because they were in bloom on February 2, the Feast of the Purification of the Virgin Mary, hence the name "Candlemas Bell" mentioned above.

On Candlemas Day, Mary's statue was taken from the altar, and snowdrops, "emblems of purity," were scattered on it. Often, too, on Candlemas a home owner would give his house the "white purification," by bringing a bowl of snowdrops into it.

As in the case of other blossoms, legends have become associated with the snowdrop. For instance, St. Francis of Assisi spoke of it as the symbol of hope. There is a story that Hope leaned over the snow-covered ground and wept because of the many flowers buried beneath it. And then, wherever her tears fell, the small snow-white flowers sprang up.

Another legend tells that when Adam and Eve were being expelled from the Garden of Eden, a snowstorm was in progress. To comfort Eve, the angel told her that spring would follow after winter had passed. Then he leaned down, touched some of the snowflakes, and changed them into delicate white snowdrops.

This flower was believed by some persons to be an emblem of death. In English rural sections the snowdrop was not in good repute. And it was thought unlucky to carry the first spray of the season into the house.

February

When in the zodiac, the fish wheel round,
They loose the floods and irrigate the ground.
Then husbandmen renew their wonted toil,
Yoke their strong steers and plow the yielding soil . . .
Yet February suns' uncertain shine,
For rain and frost alternately combine
To stop the plow, with sudden wintry storms—
And often fearful violence the month deforms.
                                        —EDMUND SPENSER

FEBRUARY, the Roman "Month of Purification"—our second month—gets its name from the Latin word, *Februarius*, through the verb, *februare*, meaning to "expiate" or "purify." At the Festival of Februa celebrated on February 15 the people repented of their wrongdoing, and offered sacrifices to their gods.

Once the noted writer Ovid wrote of this festival:

> In ancient times purgations had the name
> Of Februa, various customs prove the same . . .
> The Grecians held that pure lustrations could
> Efface an impious deed, or guilt of blood . . .

By "lustrations," Ovid meant "propitiatory offerings."

It is said that the word, *Februarius* was associated with *Februus*," a name given Faunus. He was identified with Pan, "the god of purification and fertility in man and beast." In February, during the

Feast of Lupercalia, women were purified by the priests. Such officials would walk around the streets and when they met a woman, they struck her with goatskin thongs to assure fertility and easy delivery. On February 21, the Romans also celebrated the Feast of Feralia, public religious rites, honoring the dead. Therefore, this month was an important one in Roman life.

At first, February was not in their calendar which had only ten months. Then, about 700 B.C., Numa Pompilius (the second Roman king, following Romulus) changed the year of 304 days to a lunar one of 355. He added two months: January, at the beginning of the new year; and February, at the end. Numa gave this month twenty-nine days, with thirty in Leap Year.

Later, in 452 B.C., the Decemvirs inserted February between January and March. Then, when Augustus Caesar changed the name of the month from Sextilis to August to honor himself, he took a day from February, leaving it normally with twenty-eight. He did this, so that *his* month could have as many days as July, named for Julius Caesar. Consequently, February has remained the shortest month of our year.

According to an early writer named Versteegen, the Anglo-Saxons called the second month, "Kale-monath." "Kale," or "kele," meant the "kele-wort" (now termed "cole-wort") or cabbage. This vegetable was used in making the soup which was the chief dish on the farmer's winter menu. Since cabbage was the first vegetable to sprout in February, it got the name, "sprout-kele"; and February was named for it. The Anglo-Saxons also called it "Solmoneth," and sometimes "Pancake Month"; for at this time these pagans offered gifts of cakes to the sun god.

In his book *Months*, Leigh Hunt described its characteristics:

. . . if February were not the precursor of spring, it would be the least pleasant season of the year, November not excepted. The thaws then take place; and a clammy mixture of moisture and cold succeeds which is the most disagreeable of wintry sensations.

In spite of its variable weather, poets seem to have enjoyed writing about February; for example, William Hone, in his miscellany, *The Everyday Book and Year Book,* quotes from other poets:

> All around looks sad and dreary,
> Fast the flaky snow descends;
> Yet the red-breast chirrups cheerily,
> While the mitten'd lass attends.

> Then came cold February sitting
> In an old wagon, for he could not ride,
> Drawn by two fishes . . .
> —EDMUND SPENSER

And another poet gave his version of the February weather:

> Now shifting gales and milder influence blow,
> Cloud over skies, and melt the falling snow;
> The softened earth with fertile moisture teems
> And, freed from icy bonds, down rush the swelling streams.

Thus February, from ancient times, was mentioned as a period of uncertain weather and temperatures, along with heavy rainfall. There was an early English belief that the type of weather that occurred on February 12, 13, and 14 would indicate what it would be the rest of the year.

In *The Country Almanac,* February 1676, these lines appeared:

> Foul weather is no news; hail, rain, and snow
> Are now expected, and esteemed no woe;
> Nay, 'tis an omen bad, the yeomen say,
> If Phoebus shows his face the second day.

Of course, this last line—an allusion to the sun god—refers to an old European superstition, which was brought to America and which is still widely accepted, especially in Pennsylvania. The belief was that if the sun shone on Candlemas Day (commonly termed Groundhog Day) February 2, and the little groundhog saw his shadow when he ventured out of his winter hole then there would be six more weeks of cold weather. Therefore, a cloudy, rainy day on the second of February was welcomed by farmers; for they firmly believed it foretold the early coming of the spring season.

John Clare in his *Shepherd's Calendar* for the month of February gives a happy picture of life among the milkmaids—quite a contrast to the way in which other poets had written:

> The milkmaid singing leaves her bed
> As glad as happy thoughts can be;
> While magpies chatter o'er her head,
> As jocund in the change is she.
> The cows around the closes stray,
> Nor lingering wait the foddering boy,
> Tossing the molehills in their play,
> And staring round with frolic joy.

Since many famous Americans were born in February, others consider it an honor to have arrived during this second month of the year. Someone once remarked that the trademark, "Born in February," is a real distinction. Such persons share honors with three Presidents: George Washington, William Henry Harrison, and Abraham Lincoln. All over the U.S.A. schools, churches and other organizations plan special programs on February 12, to honor Lincoln, and on the 22nd, Washington's birthday.

Other notables born in February include Charles Dickens, Horace Greeley, John Ruskin, Charles Lamb, Thomas A. Edison, James Russell Lowell, Frédéric Chopin, Victor Hugo, Henry Wadsworth Longfellow, Victor Herbert, Felix Mendelssohn, Charles Lindbergh, and Buffalo Bill Cody, as well as Gioacchino Rossini, Joseph Jefferson, Samuel Pepys, Adelina Patti, William Allen White, Charles Darwin, Louis Agassiz, Edna St. Vincent Millay, Mark Hopkins, Daniel Boone, and Sidney Lanier.

Our second month has its full share of important events: in 1635 America's first public school was opened; 1678 saw the publication of Bunyan's *Pilgrim's Progress;* in 1778 there was the first foreign salute to the Stars and Stripes; 1791 witnessed the first meeting of the U.S. Supreme Court; in 1791 John Wesley preached his last sermon; in 1815 Napoleon escaped from Elba; in 1832 Samuel Colt patented his famous six-shooter; in 1848 the U.S. made a treaty with Mexico in regard to California; in 1854 the Republican Party met for the first time; in 1861 Lincoln gave his noted Farewell speech to his home town, Springfield, Illinois; in 1862 came the publication of the song, "Battle Hymn of the Republic"; that same year greenbacks were printed for the first time; and in 1867 the first passenger train ran from Chicago to Council Bluffs, Iowa.

Other interesting February happenings: in 1870 the U.S. Weather Bureau was started; in 1885 came the dedication of the Washington Monument in the national capital; in 1897 the P.T.A. was founded; in 1910 the Boy Scouts received their charter; in 1913 occurred the ratification of the 16th Amendment to the Constitution, setting up the income tax; in 1915 the cornerstone was laid in Washington for the Lincoln Memorial; in 1919 the American Legion was founded in Paris; in 1924 Woodrow Wilson died; in 1926 the U.S. Post Office issued the first air mail stamps; in 1931 Edison's "talkies" were heard for the first time; in 1952 Elizabeth II was crowned Queen of England at Westminster Abbey; and in February 1962 the orbital flight of Lt. Col. John H. Glenn made news.

Like other months, February has its special days. On the second, some churches observe the religious holiday Candlemas with the blessing and distribution of candles; while on the same date, in certain localities, humorous celebrations take place on Groundhog Day, when weather predictions are made. The 14th of February has long been observed as St. Valentine's Day, when countless love messages and comical greetings are exchanged.

And when Leap Year comes around—only once in four years—February 29 is a very special day for those born on this date. It is estimated that about 100,000 Americans (and perhaps 2,000,000 people in the world) celebrate birthdays on February 29.

February Birthstone—Amethyst

The February birthstone is the amethyst, the purple variety of quartz, which contains traces of manganese and iron. From times of antiquity, the amethyst has been prized as a gem stone. Although it reached the zenith of its popularity during the last century, it now seems to be coming back into favor.

"Amethyst" comes from the Greek word *amethythios*, meaning "without drunkenness," and the gem was worn to cure intoxication. However, wine cups, beautifully carved from large crystals of amethyst, were used in early times in some places.

Amethysts come in varied hues; some are a clear purple, mixed with red, others are of bluish-violet crystallized quartz. Shades may vary from light lavender to dark purple or almost black. Some gems are patchy and irregular in shade. It is said that the deeper the color, the less brilliant the gem, and that ancient engravers used only the lighter stones in carrying on their craft.

These stones are found in different kinds of rock, sometimes in gravel in streams, or in volcanic terrain. Because of their abundance, amethysts are not so valuable as their beauty might lead one to believe. Some of these gems have been found in almost every country. Especially fine specimens—of deep rich purple hues known as Siberian amethysts—come from the Ural Mountains, near Ekaterinburg. The Brazilian varieties have good colors, as do those found in Uruguay. Ceylon and Madagascar are also good sources for excellent amethysts.

In the United States they have been mined in several different regions including places in Maine, Pennsylvania, North Carolina, and on the northern shore of Lake Superior.

There is an interesting old legend as to how the amethyst originated. Bacchus, the god of wine, had offended Diana. He was angry and declared he would let his tigers destroy the first person he met. This happened to be the maiden, Amethyst, who was on her way to worship at Diana's temple.

When she saw his fierce animals, she called on the goddess to save her. At once, before his eyes, Amethyst became a white statue. Then, the deity feeling repentant for his cruel intentions, poured wine over the image, and thus gave it the "crushed grape color," which makes this stone so distinctive.

We read of the amethyst in the Bible, for it was listed as the ninth gem in the breastplate worn by the Jewish high priest. It was the stone dedicated to the tribe of Dan, and symbolized judgment, courage, and justice.

In Egypt, the amethyst was popular with the Pharaohs. One of these rulers wore an ancient amulet, set with an exquisite purple stone. This particular gem is said to be in the Louvre Museum in Paris. Cleopatra used an amethyst as her signet; Catherine the Great of Russia favored this jewel; and several of the stones are set in the British coronet regalia. Tradition tells that St. Valentine wore an amethyst engraved with a figure of Cupid. When Napoleon was on his Russian campaign, he came into possession of an amethyst with the likeness of Emperor Trajan carved on it.

For many centuries this gem has been associated with religion, and often an amethyst (called the "bishop's stone") was mounted in the ecclesiastical ring worn by a bishop or other high church dignitary.

Through the ages several beliefs became connected with this attractive stone. For examples: there was the superstition that if a person owned one of these gems on which the name of the sun or moon was engraved, and wore it suspended around his neck on baboon's hair or on swallow feathers, he would be secure from storms, intemperance, and attacks by thieves. Pleasant dreams, too, were assured the individual who wore an amethyst. Many Roman ladies cherished the idea that wearing this stone would aid them in keeping their husband's affections.

In England, Edward the Confessor was the owner of a large amethyst—now mounted in one of the British crowns—which was said to have prevented his contracting contagious diseases. Cleopatra believed the gem had magical powers. Worn as an amulet, the stone would protect a person from witchcraft; it had the ability to calm men in time of battle, and had a soothing effect upon both the eyes and the spirit. Thus, this gem was not only valued for its beautiful appearance, but was favored because of its supposed supernatural powers.

February Flower—The Violet

> A violet by a mossy stone
> Half hidden from the eye;
> Fair as a star, when only one
> Is shining in the sky.
> —WILLIAM WORDSWORTH

The flower attributed to February is the violet, emblem of modesty, consequently a timid person is sometimes characterized as "a shrinking violet." John Keats once termed it the "Queen of secrecy" and Shakespeare spoke of the flowers as:

> Violets dim,
> But sweeter than the lids of Juno's eyes,
> Or Cytherea's breath.

The violet was often referred to in Greek and Roman literature, and the history of this blossom has been traced for 2,000 years from the ancient olive groves of Greece. It was the symbol of the city of Athens, just as the rose has been of England, and the lily of France. The Persians made a delicate wine from violets; and the followers of Mohammed looked upon this flower with reverence, for it was the favorite one of that prophet. Violets have long been justly popular, too, in the United States. Illinois, Wisconsin, New Jersey, and Rhode Island selected it as their state flower.

The violet, "any plant or flower of the genus Viola," comes in 300 species. It grows in temperate climes, blooms during cool weather, and is widely distributed around the globe. The plant is found both in the Northern and Southern Hemisphere, in Europe, Asia, and North America.

The ordinary hooded violet (the dogtooth, with a single purple flower) is quite common in eastern North America, from Nova Scotia to Minnesota; south to Georgia, and west to Kansas. It blooms during April, May, and June. About 80 species are found on our continent, some as far south as Costa Rica.

Each bloom has five oval petals, two that stand up, and one at each side, with a wider petal at the bottom. The short stemmed plant is rarely more than five inches tall, and the leaves are heart-shaped. Some violets are single, others, double; in varying colors of white, purple, and yellow. The plants are dormant during the winter; when spring comes, they add much beauty to the country-side.

Wild varieties are not so fragrant as those cultivated in gardens, where bees are attracted by their nectar.

"Sweet violets" are said to be native to Western Asia and lands around the Mediterranean, from which they were taken to other localities. These deep-blue flowers were the parents of cultivated varieties of today, according to some authorities. (The "true" sweet violet must be wintered in a hot house.)

The story goes that an early queen of France, Radegonde, started a convent at Poitiers. In its garden she grew sweet violets sent her by Bishop Fortunatus, who spoke of them in these words:

. . . the nobleness of the purple violet; they shine in royal purple, and perfume and beauty unite in their petals.

According to one source, the distinctive type known as "Parma" violets originally came from Turkey and the East via Italy; others believe they may have been brought from the old Moorish gardens of Spain.

In primitive times violets were used in Greece for medicinal purposes. Often a compress was made from these blooms, combined with poppy seeds, to relieve sleeplessness and headaches. In 1555 one writer said that the flowers were a fine soporific; also, "a safe and gentle purgative for children." Some people even believed that violet leaves could "alleviate or cure cancer and malignant growths."

During the medieval ages violets were cultivated in many monastery gardens. They were regarded as "powerful against evil spirits" and were used to heal inflammations, relieve hoarseness, and stop thirst.

These blossoms have for centuries been important in the manufacture of perfume which was believed to stimulate love. Shakespeare referred to this in some very much-quoted lines:

> To gild refined gold, to paint the lily,
> To throw a perfume on the violet
> Is wasteful and ridiculous excess.

In Grasse, France, a noted center of the perfume industry, as many as 150 tons of violets have been used during one season. The flower is also an important ingredient in making sherbet in Syria and Turkey; and candied violets are a popular sweetmeat in some places.

The violet was Napoleon Bonaparte's favorite flower. Josephine wore them at the time of their marriage, and on each anniversary of this event Napoleon sent her a bouquet of the fragrant blossoms. Josephine developed noted gardens at Malmaison, and sent to Parma, Italy, for fine varieties to grow on her palace grounds.

When the Emperor was banished to the Island of Elba, he declared, "I will return with the violets in the spring." When the news of his escape reached Paris, it was the violet season—late in March, 1815. In Paris, which excelled in growing "sweet violets," the Emperor's way to the Tuileries was strewn with his favorite flower, and he was showered with them. On that eventful day many ladies wore violet-hued costumes. His followers took this blossom as their emblem of loyalty to Napoleon; and it was often a means of identifying them.

Before he was taken to St. Helena, he plucked some violets from Josephine's grave; and it is said that these faded blooms were found in a locket he was wearing at the time of his death. His love for the flowers that had grown on his native island of Corsica made them very popular in France during his régime.

For some time after his passing violets were no longer popular in France, and one famous actor was hissed when he came on the stage wearing such flowers. But they came back into favor when Empress Eugenie showed her preference for them. She, like Josephine, chose them for her wedding bouquet; and in England, violets were the beloved flower of Queen Alexandra, wife of Edward VII. Earlier in Great Britain, during the rule of James I, it was customary to use violets as medicine for such purposes as:

. . . to cool any heat of the body . . . inflammation of the eyes . . . to drink the decoction of the leaves and flowers made with water or wine, or to apply them as poultices to the affected parts.

An almost forgotten English lady gardener, Jane Loudon (1807–1854), was the wife of the noted botanist and gardener, John Loudon. She has recently been brought to public attention by Bea Howe in her delightful book, *The Lady with the Green Fingers*.

Jane was not only a devoted gardener who enjoyed cultivating her garden at their home in Porchester Terrace, Bayswater, but she also interested many other Englishwomen of her era in raising flowers through several books and numerous magazine pieces she wrote on her favorite subject.

The Loudons' home was a gathering place for several notables of the time. Jane made it very attractive with her conservatory filled with various potted plants; and in addition, cut flowers throughout the rooms. Bea Howe has said this of her parlor:

Small bowls of Neapolitan violets added their own sweet scent to the festive atmosphere of the glowing taper-lit room.

Two noted singers who loved violets were the famous tenor, Jean de Reszke, and Emma Eames. The former, when asked which woman singer with whom he had appeared in opera pleased him most, he declared it was Emma Eames, for "She was so handsome, she was such a lady, her hands were so beautiful, and she always smelled so sweetly of violets." When de Reszke died in Nice, he was buried in Montparnasse Cemetery in Paris, where his pupils covered his casket with a blanket of Parma violets.

The violet was the preferred flower of a noted American, Mrs. Jack Gardner (the "discriminating patron of the arts" and world famous collector). She grew her own violets and each day fresh ones were placed in front of her favorite painting, "Christ Bearing the Cross," by Giorgione.

Her Venetian palace, Fenway Court, in Boston, open to the public, is an outstanding gallery, containing 290 paintings, hundreds of ceramics, pieces of sculpture, and miscellaneous items. And today, according to the terms of her will that everything should be kept as in her lifetime, violets are still placed before her favorite picture.

At Athens, the populace made garlands and wreaths of these blossoms for ceremonial occasions, including marriage rites. Violets, too, were frequently placed at tombs.

There is a legend that once, when Orpheus sat down to rest on a mossy bank, the first violets sprang up from the spot where his lyre had rested. Another myth tells that Jupiter had fallen in love with Io, a priestess in Juno's temple. To save Io from the jealous wrath of the queen of the gods, Jupiter turned her into a white heifer, and then created white violets for her to eat. Later, it is said that Venus became envious when Cupid admired these flowers, and she changed the petals to dark ones.

The violet originates, according to one story, from the day that Christ was crucified; the shadow of His cross fell on several plants, including the violet which drooped in sorrow, "thereby tokening its consecration to Christian service."

References to this February flower are often found in the works of many English authors. Shakespeare, both in his plays and sonnets, mentioned violets. Once he declared they filled the March woods with fragrance. In Hamlet, the bard wrote of Ophelia:

> . . . Lay her i' the earth;
> And from her fair and unpolluted flesh
> May violets spring.

Elsewhere, Shakespeare spoke of "the violets that strew the green lap of new-come spring." Today, around Stratford-on-Avon, these well-loved flowers still grow abundantly.

Bayard Taylor once spoke of the violet as "loving a sunny bank," while May Riley Smith praised the flowers in these lines:

> Strange that we should slight the violets,
> Till the lovely flowers are gone.

Early in this century—about 1914—these blossoms began to be grown on an extensive scale for European flower markets. Now the cultivation of violets is also an important industry in America ranking third in importance in the commercial flower trade. Many fine types that are raised nowadays have been developed from a fragrant wild species that grew in the British Isles, in Siberia, the Himalayas, and near the Mediterranean. Some popular varieties are named the "Princess of Wales," "Rosina," "Czar White," and "Double Russian."

Bunches of violets are much appreciated by women, even in these days of orchids and gardenias; and in one of his poems, the modern British poet Alfred Noyes urges their purchase:

> Buy a bunch of violets for the lady,
> And tell her she's your own true love.

Alternate February Flower—Primrose

> Welcome, pale primrose! starting up between
> Dead matted leaves of ash and oak that strew
> The every lawn, the wood, and spinney through,
> Mid creeping moss and ivy's darker green . . .
> While the meek shepherd stops his simple song,
> To gaze a moment on a pleasing sight;
> O'erjoyed to see the flowers that truly bring
> The welcome news of sweet returning spring.

The alternate February flower, the primrose, is a plant of the genus *primula,* and gets its name from *primus,* meaning "first," because of its early blooming. It is sometimes called the "first flower of spring." One writer said of it, "The primrose seems the very flower of delicacy and refinement."

There are hundreds of species, mostly perennials, found in the North Temperate Zone, in North America, Europe, and Asia. Since primroses grow well in high altitudes, many have come from the mountains of Tibet and India. The wild varieties grow close to the ground, and make a fragrant yellow carpet. Finally, primroses are sweet-scented, attracting butterflies and bees.

One writer has well said:

Their fine colors and soft delicate beauty have led to the cultivation of some species; and numerous varieties and hybrid forms, with single and double flowers of various tints have been developed.

The primrose is an interesting plant, either in its wild state or when cultivated, and with its red, white, or yellow blossoms adds much to the beauty of a garden. Usually the flower is propagated by seed; and more are grown in the British Isles than in the United States. Primroses are often used in rock gardens, or as border plants, in ornamental gardens, and sometimes grown in pots in conservatories. They are also well adapted to winter shade gardens.

A favorite kind is the English primrose (although it is not confined to that country, for it is seen in much of Europe, too). It is said to have more than fifty species. This popular flower, with its golden or pale yellow petals, is often the first blossom "to dare to show its face in the chilly spring."

According to legend, the primrose was dedicated to a Sicilian martyr, St. Agatha, who died about 251 A.D. She was tortured, but refused to have a physician; so St. Peter descended from heaven, filled her prison cell with light, and healed her wounds.

Another well-known type is the evening primrose. It is a native yellow biennial, considered "the best yellow-flowered biennial for bold effects." It has a strong stem, is four or five feet tall, and bears blooms four to five inches across. This evening primrose blooms from July to October, and grows all over the country, from Canada to Florida, and west to the Pacific Coast.

One authority says that the evening primrose went from its native Virginia, in 1619, to Padua, Italy, and that it also reached England about the same time. Two years later another botanist described it as the "tree-primrose of Virginia," or the "prime-rose tree."

In the daytime the flower is a rather ordinary looking roadside plant; but when the pods, which have been closed, suddenly open at sundown, the evening primrose becomes "a luminous torch of alluringly scented pale yellow flowers." Therefore, this plant is noted for the distinctive ability to open and shut its petals regularly.

Several varieties of primrose are said to be native to California and

Patagonia. Formerly, in Germany, France, and New England, primrose roots and leaves were eaten; some people believed they would cure asthma and whooping cough. And an ointment made from this flower was used to relieve all kinds of pain.

The British have always been devoted to this simple flower; and the story is told that many years ago, when a single plant was exhibited in Melbourne, Australia, no less than 3,000 persons—many of them bushmen and rough miners—thronged to see this reminder of their far-off native land.

Benjamin Disraeli, Lord Beaconsfield, the famous British Prime Minister, cherished the primrose as his favorite blossom and at times would take Queen Victoria little gifts of primrose nosegays. When she and her ladies-in-waiting were staying at Osborne House on the Isle of Wight, they would gather primroses and ship them to Disraeli in London.

In 1882, two years after Disraeli's death, Lord Randolph Churchill and other prominent Conservatives formed an organization known as the "Primrose League," to support the great Prime Minister's principles, to spread Conservative propaganda, and "to infuse new life into the Conservative Party." One writer commented that it was rather strange that "the theatrical, sophisticated" Premier "should be commemorated by such an English flower as the primrose."

The membership of the Primrose League included men and women with the titles of Knights and Dames. The day of Lord Beaconsfield's death—April 19—was designated as "Primrose Day." On that date, members of the organization, wearing primroses, met and laid wreaths of these flowers at the foot of Disraeli's statue in London.

Primroses were also the favorites of several writers; Keats loved them, as did Goldsmith, who composed this line, "Sweet as the primrose peeps through the thorn," while Wordsworth declared of one unappreciative person:

> A primrose by a river's brim
> A yellow primrose was to him,
> And it was nothing more.

However, the early poet, John Clare, wrote this contrasting reaction:

> And while he plucked the primrose in its pride,
> He pondered o'er its bloom, 'twixt joy and pain.

Shakespeare has immortalized this flower by several well known references to it. He used the expressions, "primrose path," and "primrose way" to describe a life of pleasure. In *Macbeth* he wrote, "Go the primrose way to everlasting bonfire." In *Hamlet*, "Himself the primrose path of dalliance treads."

Robert Louis Stevenson was of the same mind in this couplet:

> Life is over, life was gay,
> We have come the primrose way.

The Greeks associated melancholy with the primrose, and from them comes this legend: a handsome youth, son of Flora and Priapus, lost his betrothed; and when he died of grief, the gods changed his body to a primrose.

During Shakespeare's time this flower was also associated with early death, as attested to in *The Winter's Tale* when Perdita says:

> . . . pale primroses that die unmarried
> Ere they behold bright Phoebus in his strength . . .

March

The stormy March has come at last
With winds and clouds and changing skies . . .
—WILLIAM CULLEN BRYANT

OUR third month, March, got its name from that of the
Roman month, "Martius," honoring Mars, the god of war. According to Ovid, he was the father of their first prince. Since wars and
conquests were such important factors in Roman life, it was only
natural for these people to dedicate a month to the deity of war.

An early writer, in William Hone's *Everyday Book* declared:

Perhaps the ascription of this month to Mars by the Romans was a
compliment to themselves; they were the sons of war and might naturally
deduce their origin from the belligerent deity . . .

Another source has this to say:

As to the deity's nature, March has certainly nothing in common with
it; for though it affects to be very rough, it is one of the best natured
months in the year, drying up the superabundant moisture of winter,
with its fierce winds, and thus restoring our paths through the fields . . .

Martius had the distinction of being the first month of the Roman
year until the adoption of the Julian Calendar in 46 B.C. Beginning
the year in March seemed logical; for as has been well said, it comes
"after the 'dead' of the year, in which symptoms of growth take
place."

In many countries beginning the year in March prevailed for centuries. France, for example, made a change in 1564, when Charles IX decreed that the French year should start on January 1. However, Great Britain and her Colonies continued to use March 25, until 1752, when an act of Parliament changed the first day of a new year to January 1. Strange to say, in some communities, the old idea persisted; and homes or farms were leased yearly, beginning on March 25.

The Saxons—so Veersteegen stated—called March "lenctmonat," or "length-moneth," or "lencten-monath," because at this time, the days began to exceed the nights in length. These people had another name, too, for March: "rhed-monath," for the goddess Rhedam, whom they honored with sacrifices in March.

Early Britons also termed March "hyld-monath," "a loud or stormy month." When the Anglo-Saxons accepted Christianity, they held their chief season of fasting at this time; it was called the "fast of lenet monet" (the Anglo-Saxon "lengten," or "lencten," meant "spring"). March was the "spring" month, so the fast became "lent."

An old saying was prevalent both in England and Scotland that March had borrowed three days from April. So the last three days of March were called the "borrowed" days.

This third month has always been noted for its varied weather. After February rains, English farmers hoped for a dry spell, in order to get their sowing and planting done. Therefore they welcomed dust during March, and such proverbs as these were current: "A dry March never begs for bread," and "a peck of March dust is worth a king's ransom."

One poet described the life of farmers during March in these terms:

> Now husbandmen and hinds in March prepare
> And order take against the teeming year.
> Survey their lands and keep a good lookout
> To get their fields and farms well fenced about.

The English writer Leigh Hunt, in *The Months,* writes this about March:

The animal creation now exhibit unequivocal signs of activity. The farmer extends the exercise of his plough, and if fair weather continues, begins sowing barley and oats. Bats and reptiles break up their winter sleep . . . Young lambs come tottering forth in mild weather . . . and lastly forth issues the bee with his vernal trumpet, to tell us there is news of sunshine and the flowers . . .

Since this month is associated with blustery winds and changeable weather, there is the old saying that March "comes in like a lion and goes out like a lamb." Once William Dean Howells wrote these lines:

> Tossing his mane of snows in wildest eddies . . .
> Lion-like March cometh in hoarse . . .

And a later poet of our day, Enola Chamberlain, has described March in this fashion:

> This is the month of winds that whirl,
> That stream and twist and turn and curl . . .
> This is the month, the month of wind,
> That piles the clouds or drives them thinned
> In reluctant herds, some low, some high,
> Relentlessly across the sky.

Helen Hunt Jackson once complimented this so-called "blustery" month:

> Ah March! we know thou art
> Kind-hearted; 'spite of ugly looks and threats,
> And, out of sight, art nursing April's violets.

And another author gives this reaction regarding our third calendar month:

March is a rude and boisterous month, possessing many of the characteristics of winter, yet awakening sensations perhaps more delicious than the two following spring months; for it gives the first announcement and taste of spring.

March has the distinction of having four Presidential birthdays—those of Andrew Jackson, James Madison, Grover Cleveland, and John Tyler.

Other well known persons born the third month include William Dean Howells, Sam Houston, Vincent Van Gogh, Knute Rockne, Alexander Graham Bell, Michaelangelo, Elizabeth B. Browning, Leland Stanford, Joseph Haydn, Robert Frost, Rosa Bonheur, General Phil Sheridan, Robert Millikin, Oliver Wendell Holmes, and William Jennings Bryan.

Also, Luther Burbank, Arturo Toscanini, Johann Sebastian Bach, David Livingston, Kate Greenaway, Albert Einstein, Robert Bruce, John C. Calhoun, and Andrew W. Mellon.

Interesting events have taken place in March; for example: in 1702 the world's first daily newspaper, *The Courant*, was established in London; in 1718 there was the first inoculation for small pox; in 1775 Patrick Henry delivered the speech containing his famous words, "Give me liberty, or give me death"; in 1780, the first American Bank was chartered; in 1781 the Constitution of the United States was ratified; in 1789, the first U.S. Congress met in New York; that same year Congress established the U.S. Post Office; in 1794 an act was passed to found our Navy; in 1802, the United States Military Academy at West Point was started; in 1819 the first bicycle was seen in New York; in 1842 ether was used for the first time; in 1852, *Uncle Tom's Cabin* was published; also that year the first cartoon of Uncle Sam appeared; in 1862 there was the famous battle of the Monitor and the Merrimac.

In 1865, Jeff Davis was captured; in 1867 the United States Bureau of Education was set up; in 1876, Alexander Graham Bell patented his telephone; in 1882, Congress passed a bill giving pensions to the widows of Presidents; in 1884, our country set up Standard Time; in 1912 the Camp Fire Girls' organization was founded; in 1917, Puerto Rico became a Territory of the U.S.A.; that same year Jeanette Rankin of Montana was elected to the House of Representatives, the first woman to hold such an office; in 1931 Congress adopted "The Star Spangled Banner" as our national anthem; in 1925 the first trans-Atlantic broadcast was made; and in 1938 Adolf Hitler invaded Austria.

March does not have so many widely observed holidays as some other months. St. David's Day, in honor of the patron saint of Wales falls on March first.

The "wearing of the green" by the Irish and by countless Americans is in great evidence on St. Patrick's Day, March 17. This date commemorates the death of St. Patrick rather than his birth. The Irish parade proudly, especially in New York City, honoring their patron saint, and all over the country Americans enjoy getting together for St. Patrick's Day dinners or other parties.

Since Easter is a movable feast, it may fall between March 22 and April 25. According to a table of Easter dates for this century, about one-fourth of them will occur in March, and the rest in April.

March Birthstone—Bloodstone

The March birthstone—the bloodstone—is sometimes called "St. Stephen's stone." It is a closely compact opaque variety of quartz, with a background color of dark green, mottled with irregular spots and streaks of red.

A semi-precious gem with a waxy lustre, it has also been found in other colors such as yellow, gray, and black. At times the stone contains bands of varying hues, or markings that form natural pictures.

The ancients called the bloodstone "jasper"; it was one of the gems in the breastplate of the High Priest. And in the *Book of Revelation* (21:19) we read that jasper was used in the first foundation of the city of New Jerusalem.

The bloodstone occurs in large masses (sometimes embedded in rock), as well as in the form of pebbles. Stones of the highest quality come from India and the Ural Mountains. One fine translucent variety—the heliotrope—is native to India only. Siberia, the

New Hebrides, and Canada also produce these gems. In the United States, they have been discovered in Chatham County, Georgia; Orange County, New York; and in the states of California and Oregon.

In Great Britain, the common name for the bloodstone is "heliotrope." Tradition says the name came from the belief that such a gem was placed in water, in a container that had been rubbed with juice of the heliotrope plant. When the vessel was exposed to the rays of the sun, the water appeared red, and "the sun, bloodlike, as if eclipsed."

Sources, however, vary as to how the bloodstone got its name. One authority says it came, not from the color of the gem, but from an old belief that such a stone could stop bleeding. Some ancients declared it was the stone that lay under the cross of Christ at Calvary, and that, as He hung there, it became stained with His blood. Another version is that the drops of blood fell from the dripping sword of a Roman soldier at Golgotha upon a piece of dark green jasper. Italians still call the gem "bloody jasper."

Because the bloodstone is quite hard and takes a fine polish, it was popular material on which to carve sacred objects, and was highly regarded, especially by Byzantine artists, because of its supposed origin at Christ's cross.

Interesting scenes of the Crucifixion have been engraved on bloodstones. Early artists also depicted other sacred events on these gems, many of which were used in signet rings. During the nineteenth century, Russian lapidaries engraved designs on jasper from Siberia. They also made varied objects of art from these stones.

Beautiful antique articles in unusual designs fashioned from bloodstones can still be seen in outstanding gem collections. Such objects of art include seal rings, intaglios, cameos, small vases, and statues. Large pieces of bloodstone have been made into clock frames and trinket boxes.

Early Babylonians and Egyptians used these stones as amulets. Spaniards, Mexicans, and Indians in New Spain cut such gems into the shape of hearts and wore them to guard against diseases of this organ. There were beliefs, too, that a bloodstone could heal inflammatory illnesses; stop anger and discord; make water boil; also that the streaks, because of their association with blood, could cause bleeding to cease by a single touch of the gem. Some early astronomers even declared this stone helped in the detection and observation of the eclipse of the sun.

Since the bloodstone was believed to bring its wearer popularity, courage, and wisdom; and in addition, could protect all those born in March, it is not surprising that it was selected as birthstone for this month.

Alternate March Birthstone—Aquamarine

The alternate March birthstone is the lovely aquamarine, also known as beryl. It is a native silicate of aluminum and the light metal, beryllium, and has the same chemical composition as an emerald. Such stones are often embedded in large crystals. Some are fairly flawless, but many have imperfections and cannot be sold as perfect gems.

Aquamarines and other varieties of beryl are found in larger stones, and in great quantities. Considering the beauty of aquamarines, they are indeed modest in price, costing far less than emeralds.

Their romantic, poetic name means "sea water." These gems are transparent and translucent, and vary in hue from pale blue to deep blue and there is also a bluish-green variety. Lighter ones cost less than the deep blue type, which are, in truth, as rare as emeralds. Aquamarines are usually homogeneous in shade, and retain their natural colors when exposed to artificial light.

In ancient times, lovers of these stones (including Egyptians, Greeks, and Romans) obtained them mostly from several places in India, such as Madras, Rajputana, and Kashmir. When Pliny (Roman naturalist, A.D. 23–79) was writing about precious stones, he said

. . . the lovely aquamarine, which seems to have come from some mermaid's treasure house, in the depths of a summer sea, has charms not to be denied.

Today the chief places where aquamarines are found are the Ural Mountains, Russian Siberia, South Africa, Madagascar (which has produced some splendid specimens of the lighter types), and Brazil. This stone is found also in the British Isles; and a deep blue variety, embedded in granite, comes from the Mourne Mountains in County Downe, Ireland.

In recent years, most of the largest and finest aquamarines have originated in Brazil, where they are said to be the most popular of gem stones. One of the most abundant Brazilian sources is Minas Gerais, where stones of clear transparent blues, greens, and yellows are found in large numbers. Blue aquamarines of exceptional quality are found on the Mucuri.

The largest recorded gem quality stone of this type was discovered in Brazil on March 28, 1910, in a pegmatite vein, at a depth of 15 feet. It weighed 243 pounds, was of a bluish color, and measured 19 by 16 inches. In form, this aquamarine was that of a slightly irregular prism. The gem was so transparent one could see through it from end to end. The owners took it to Bahia, where it is said to have been sold for the sum of $25,000.

The United States has also produced some of these attractive stones—the richest colored ones having come from Royalston, in Massachusetts; Haddam, Connecticut; and Stoneham, Maine. Such gems have also been discovered at Mesa Grande, in San Diego County, California, and in North Carolina.

American attention was first drawn—so it is said—to the aquamarine in 1906. Vice-President William H. Taft gave a lovely stone of this kind to Alice Roosevelt, daughter of President Theodore Roosevelt, when she married Nicholas Longworth.

In 1937 the Brazilian government presented President Franklin D. Roosevelt a large stone of rare quality; and in 1953 this same South American country gave Queen Elizabeth II a superb necklace of aquamarines.

In olden days, these gems were used for dagger handles and in various other ways. It is easy for engravers to work with this comparatively soft stone; and several fine examples of their artistry have been found. Today the lovely hued gems are used in larger pieces of jewelry, in pendants, earrings, and especially as finger rings.

One writer declared that no special virtues have been attributed to the aquamarine and that it is highly desirable for its beauty alone. However, another source states that among some people at one time, there was a belief that this stone would protect its owner from the perils of the sea and endow her with the spirit of youth and fascination. There was also a saying that the gem in powdered form was a sure cure for laziness.

March Flower—Jonquil or Daffodil

> Daffodils
> That come before swallows dare, and take
> The winds of March with beauty.

Thus Shakespeare in *The Winter's Tale* praised the daffodil, and centuries later William Wordsworth penned these familiar lines:

> When all at once I saw a crowd,
> A host of dancing daffodils
> Beside the lake, beneath the trees,
> Fluttering and dancing in the breeze.

Those born in March may use either the jonquil or daffodil as their birthmonth flower. Since both have yellow flowers and bloom in the spring, jonquils and daffodils are frequently confused.

The two are closely related to the narcissus; in fact, "narcissus" is the botanical name for the entire family. One writer has said that "any narcissus is a daffodil; that narcissus is used by botanists, and daffodil by gardeners." (See Narcissus in Chapter 12.)

The jonquil, which announces "the advent of a mild and genuine spring," is a bulbous plant, with a cluster of small, either single or double, bright yellow, fragrant flowers. Its blooms hang from one stem; the tube is slender and less than an inch long; and the narrow, glossy, dark-green leaves are rush-like.

The name, "jonquil," comes from a Spanish word, *junquillo*, meaning "a little rush." The common jonquil, a plant up to eight inches in height, is said to have been a native of Southern Europe and Algeria. It has long been popular in the British Isles, and double jonquils were planted in the gardens around Blenheim Castle when those grounds were first laid out.

Some sources affirm that jonquils have never been quite so well-liked as daffodils, although they have been steady favorites with many gardeners; and numerous varieties have been extensively cultivated.

The name, "daffodil," was formerly given to several bulbous plants including a white narcissus, and the "checquered daffodil," an early spring flowering bulb with a single flower on its stem.

The word itself—"daffodil"—has an interesting origin. It is said to be a corruption of *asphodelus*, meaning "the king's spear." The word was slurred, and in turn became "affodylle," "affodil," "dafo-dil," and "daffy-down-dilly." When English children saw the meadows covered with these yellow blossoms, they would sing:

> Daffo-down dill has come to town
> In a yellow petticoat and a green gown.

This flower, "the showiest and most easily grown . . . of the genus Narcissus has 50 species and well defined varieties." It has a single stalk and broad leaves; and its trumpet is longer than the petals. One of the best and earliest is the "King Alfred," which has been cultivated in gardens for many years.

The daffodil is a hardy and widely spread plant, which grew wild in the woods and fields of Morocco, Spain, and other Mediterranean lands, as well as in northern Europe, including England and Wales. In the old Chinese Empire, the daffodil was the emblem of spring, and called the "sacred Lily of China" and the "Flower of the Gods."

In early times attempts were made to concoct an ointment from daffodil blossoms, but this was not successful. The sap contains calcium oxalate crystals, which make the leaves disagreeable, and may be harmful to animals. In certain cases it has caused a skin rash just by picking the blooms.

The leek—so it is said—was the Welsh emblem ever since the Battle of Agincourt, and was worn on St. David's Day in Wales. Henry Tudor's colors were green and white; his adherents picked leeks and wore them to show their loyalty, while the opposition used daffodils. After a long rivalry, the latter won out.

One source notes that the Gaelic word, *cenin*, referred both to the leek and the daffodil. The latter is much more plentiful in Wales than the leek. In 1911, when Edward VIII (now Duke of Windsor) was proclaimed Prince of Wales, the Welsh adopted the daffodil as their national flower.

Iris Lewis, a native of Wales, once wrote that it was a Welsh custom to wear a daffodil on the first day of March. Many families grew their own, and everyone tried to have them blooming for this date. Once, when the flowers hadn't bloomed yet at her home, Iris and her sister hesitated about appearing at school without the customary blossoms. Luckily for them, a neighbor girl came along with some extra ones, and so saved the day for the two sisters.

The common or wild daffodil, sometimes called the "Lenten Lily," with a single yellow bloom, once grew in such profusion in the environs of London that the flower women went out in the meadows, gathered the flowers, and sold them on the streets of London.

In Elizabethan gardens daffodils were carefully nourished, as they were much loved by the people of that time. Many varieties were brought to the British Isles from different parts of the Continent to be grown by garden-lovers.

Early in the sixteenth century William Turner is said to have written the first published description of the daffodil. He had an outstanding garden near where the famous Kew Gardens are now located. In Turner's time there were about twenty different kinds known; but by 1629 about 200 varieties were being cultivated. The Dean of Manchester Cathedral, William Herbert, was an early grower of daffodils, and in 1837 he wrote a book about these flowers.

In the British Isles and other parts of Europe there was much competition in raising daffodils, and often fantastic prices were paid for the bulbs. In 1863 Peter Barr and a friend began to concentrate on raising such plants and soon Barr was being called "The Daffodil King." Once he made a journey to Spain to find wild ones that would grow in English gardens. In 1884 he was one of the sponsors of a daffodil conference. Until Barr's death in 1909, he was unexcelled in "growing, selecting, crossing, and improving the daffodil." His work was continued by George H. Engleheart, dubbed the "Father of the Modern Daffodil."

The first daffodil show was held in Birmingham, England, in 1893. Ever since, these flowers have made good progress and are now among the most popular in the world. Since the beginning of the century, numerous new types have been developed.

Daffodils are grown in large quantities in the United States, and are highly esteemed early bloomers. One place connected with daffodils, widely known as "Daffodil Hill," is in Amador County, California, near Volcano, an old Gold Rush mining town.

During the 1850's, the golden blossoms which have made this spot famous were brought west in covered wagons. Since then they have kept multiplying; and now, each spring, from about the middle of March until the end of April the area is a great mass of golden yellow, with more than one hundred varieties in evidence. Many flower-lovers travel long distances to see this beautiful, distinctive sight. Those whose hobby is taking colored slides or films have a field day when "Daffodil Hill" can be seen and photographed in all its glory. The well-known California writer, Wallace Stegner once said:

Daffodils are an odd ending, a quaint consequence of the human flood that rushed to California and stayed to build a state and a society.

It is a delight to drive through the Mother Lode district in the spring. This part of the country seems to be outstandingly suited to growing daffodils. The rains come in the winter, and during the dry summers, the plants get the rest needed for their proper growth. As much of the land is sloping, the bulbs have the right drainage. Many ranchers feature daffodils in their gardens, and in fields and on hillsides, you can see the yellow blossoms that in some cases are the only remains of the sites of early ranch homes.

In this region, about two miles from the old town of Diamond Springs and about five miles from Placerville, Iola Sweet Young, after years of hard work and loving care, has created an outstanding daffodil garden. When she and her husband Robert built their home on a knoll on the Pleasant Valley Road, she decided she would have a daffodil garden although up to that time she had not had much experience in this line.

Mrs. Young literally started from scratch and has been at it faithfully ever since. She fashioned stone steps down the slope and made small terraces in which she planted her first daffodils—the ordinary kind that had been growing on the ranch.

One day when in town she bought some "store" bulbs. At the same time she began to study catalogues and was amazed at the number and variety of these flowers. At first she ordered moderately priced bulbs, but as years passed, she indulged in some really choice ones. Year by year she has added more terraces and beds with paths between them.

Although she is quite creative, when she started her garden she had no special plan, so like Topsy, "it just grew." However, the total result is pleasing, and the terraces extend gracefully down the sloping knoll.

She has now become a bit "choosy," and often weeds out the less distinctive bulbs. These she shares with appreciative neighbors and friends. About every three years Mrs. Young separates and replants. Now her garden is quite extensive and contains about 150 different kinds of daffodils. When the flowers are in bloom she has many visitors to see the beautiful blossoms which she generously shares with others. Each spring her garden club has a charming "Daffodil Tea," which is an outstanding event in the community.

On the Pacific Coast daffodils are highly prized; and some places hold annual exhibits of these plants. The Southern California Daffodil Societies meet at the famed Descanso Gardens where a trophy, a sterling silver hand wrought bowl, is awarded the best collection of seven varieties of five stems each. This competition started back in 1938.

Each year at the University of California at Berkeley, one fraternity puts on its Daffodil Festival for which a queen is chosen. Recently the candidates for the honor of being queen and the fraternity members sold daffodils and gave the proceeds to help needy students in Ceylon.

These gay flowers never fail to please the eye and one writer, Carl Maskey, has said of them:

Daffodils bring with them the colors that brighten up any part of the garden. They may be used in a natural setting, in containers, and both inside and outdoors. They are equally appealing planted in beds preceding annuals which bloom later in the year.

Recently, in regard to daffodils (sometimes called the "trumpets of spring") an authority, Edward Gottlieb, stated that there are more than 10,000 registered named varieties. Dutch growers who supply the majority of the bulbs, suggest that gardeners become acquainted with the major classes.

Varieties come and go: now several that were once favorites are obsolete. Mr. Gottlieb said that some kinds bloom earlier than others, while certain types multiply faster than others.

Here is the outline of the major divisions as given by him:

TRUMPET DAFFODILS: These have the long cup and are prized for their size. They include the yellow "King Alfred" and the "Unsurpassable," also the white "Mount Hood" and "Beersheba."

LARGE CUPPED DAFFODILS: Sometimes the cup is colored and the petals white as in "Fortune," "Flower Record," or "Mrs. R. O. Backhouse."

SMALL CUPPED DAFFODILS: In these the cups are smaller than the petals; examples: "Edward Buxton," "Verger," and "Chinese White."

DOUBLE DAFFODILS: Examples; "Inglescombe," "Texas," and "Mary Copeland."

TRIANDRUS HYBRIDS: These are always white, with as many as six flowers on the stem. "Thalia" is the best known.

CYCLAMINEUS HYBRIDS: The dwarf flowers include "Baby Doll" and "February Gold."

JONQUILLA HYBRIDS: Known for their fragrance, they often are pale-yellow, as in the "Trevithian."

TAZETTA (sometimes called "poetaz"): They have a wide range of colors; examples are "Laurens Koster," "Cheerfulness," "Scarlet Gem," and "Yellow Cheerfulness."

POETICUS: These have white petals with yellow cups, edged with orange or red, as in "Actea."

And from time immemorial noted poets have sung eloquently about the charms of daffodils. Homer wrote of them in his *Hymn to Demeter;* and Shakespeare, in *The Winter's Tale,* declared:

> When daffodils begin to peer
> With heigh! the doxy over the dale,
> Why, then comes in the sweet o' the year . . .

Other important British bards, including Spenser, Keats, Tennyson and Wordsworth have sung their praises, as have some contemporary poets who have used these flowers as their subjects. For instance, Robert Loveman wrote this couplet:

> It is not raining rain to me,
> It's raining daffodils . . .

John Masefield, England's noted Poet Laureate, declared that "April's in the west wind and daffodils." A. E. Housman advised his friends:

> . . . And bear from hill and valley
> The daffodil away . . .

And another modern British poet, W. W. Gibson, has given us an unforgettable picture:

> Moon-pale daffodils under the April moon . . .
> The silence and wonder of daffodils dancing by moonlight.

Today daffodils are as popular as ever in England. If you are lucky enough to visit some of the stately homes now open to the public, in the spring you may see great stretches of these flowers. For example, at Chatsworth (the home of the Duke of Devonshire, in Derbyshire) the daffodils bloom abundantly along a small lake in front of the castle.

April

In April in old calendars is drawn
A gallant hawker, pacing on a lawn,
Holding a bell'd and hooded fowl of prey,
Ready to loose him in the airy way,
For daily now, ascends the solar beam,
And the warm earth seems in a waking dream;
Insects creep out, levees burst, and flowers rise.
And buds enchant the woods and wing the skies . . .
　　　　　　　　—EDMUND SPENSER

AT first, our fourth month, April, was the second one in the Roman calendar, until Numa Pompilius added two more months: January and February. Originally, too, April had 29 days; later, Julius Caesar added one to it, making 30.

The meaning and origin of the word, "April," seem to be subjects of considerable debate. Several dictionaries say it is derived from the Latin term, *Aprilis*. In ancient times it was customary to name months for deities; April was sacred to Venus, and her festival—the Festum Veneris and Fortuna Virilis—occurred on the first day of this month. As a result, some conjectured that *Aprilis* stems from *aphrilis*, corrupted from *Aphrodite*, the Greek name for Venus. However, one authority, Jakob Grimm, opposed this, stating it may have originated from the name of a hypothetical god or hero named *Aper* or *Aprus*.

Others have asserted that "April" comes from a Latin verb *aperire* denoting "to open," referring to the opening of leaves and buds at this season. This seems a logical conclusion. However, since no other month has been named for natural conditions or circumstances, some sources have ruled out this suggestion.

Since the first day of April was consecrated to Venus, the "Goddess of Beauty," "Mother of Love," "Queen of Laughter," "Mistress of the Grapes," on this date Roman ladies performed certain rites under myrtle trees. They made and wore crowns of myrtle leaves and offered sacrifices to Venus. It is said that widows and virgins met at the temple of Fortuna Virilis, and "disclosing their personal deformities, prayed the goddess to conceal them from their husbands."

Romans also observed other festivals during April, including games, the Ludi Megalenses, in honor of the deity Cybele, "the great nature goddess of the ancient peoples of Asia Minor." On the 21st day of this month, the birthday of the city of Rome was celebrated; and at these ceremonies—the Vinalia Urbana—wine made the preceding fall was tasted for the first time. Then, beginning on April 28 and continuing for five days, Romans celebrated the Floralia, in honor of Flora, the deity of flowers.

In Charlemagne's calendar, April was known as "Grass-month"; the Anglo-Saxons called it "Oster-monath," or "Eostur-monath," for Eostre (Ostra, or Eastre), goddess of the spring, whose festival they observed each year. The Christian celebration of Christ's Resurrection took its name from the Anglo-Saxon term.

In ancient pictures April was sometimes shown as a young girl dressed in green; in one hand she was holding garlands of hawthorn and myrtle, with violets and roses in the other.

Primitive peoples always enjoyed the month of April because of the longed-for arrival of spring. In 1661 a writer spoke of it as "the jewel of time and the joy of nature." His glowing description of April, found in *The Twelve Months*, contained these words:

The youth of the country make ready for the morris dance, and the merry milkmaid supplies them with ribbons her true love has given her

. . . The aged feel a kind of youth . . . and the youthful cheeks are as red as a cherry.

Also in *The Mirror of Months*, another gave his reaction to the arrival of our fourth month:

April is spring—the only spring which we possess—the most juvenile of the months; and the most feminine—the sweetest month of the year; partly because it ushers in the May, and partly for its own sake.
Since the business of creation begins anew in this month,
. . . the vital spark rekindles in dormant existences; and all things live and move and have their being . . . the earth puts on her livery to await the call of her lord; the air breathes gently on his cheek, and conducts to his ear the warblings of the birds and the odors of new-born herbs and flowers.

The old saying, "April showers bring May flowers" has long been a familiar one, for this month is associated with the idea of frequent rains. Someone has characterized April as having "showers and sunshine rapidly chasing each other." Such rainy weather was welcomed by one poet because

> An April flood
> Carries away the frog and his brood.

And another unnamed poet has given us this quatrain:

> Sunshine intermits with ardor,
> Shades fly swiftly o'er the fields;
> Showers revive the drooping verdure
> Sweets the sunny upland yields.

April, like March, has been noted for winds, as shown in this bit of early verse:

> When April blows his horn,
> It's good for both hay and corn.

In the Northern Hemisphere, April weather has often been so variable that its name has become almost synonymous with fickleness. The month often has extremes—both hot and cold days, as well as rain and sunshine. Once Shakespeare declared:

> O! how this spring of love resembleth
> The uncertain glory of an April day.

Two twentieth-century poets have also written of this characteristic:

> Willows drip a green-gold rain
> In April's frequent showers.
>   —GLADYS ROOT SWARTZ

> Beckoning from blue or stormy skies,
> April smiles, and then April sighs . . .
>   —LOUISE BATES

Our fourth month has given us four Presidents: James Buchanan, Thomas Jefferson, James Monroe, and Ulysses S. Grant. Other interesting personalities born in April include Raphael, Charlemagne, Hans Christian Andersen, Richard II, Washington Irving, Catherine of Russia, Booker T. Washington, the Duke of Wellington, Mary Pickford, Joseph Pulitzer, Jean Jacques Rousseau, Samuel F. B. Morse, Adolf Hitler, Elizabeth II, and Yehudi Menuhin. Leonardo da Vinci, Oliver Cromwell, John Muir, F. W. Woolworth, Henry Clay, Alonzo Stagg, James J. Audubon, and Queen Juliana of the Netherlands.

April has a full quota of important events to its credit: in 1513 Ponce de Leon discovered Florida; in 1616 Shakespeare died; in 1759 Handel conducted his last performance of the Messiah; in 1775 Paul Revere made that noted midnight ride; in 1790 the U.S. Patent System was founded; in 1792 Congress established the U.S. Mint; in 1800 the Library of Congress opened; in 1830 the Mormon Church (Latter Day Saints) was established; in 1833 the first soda fountain was patented; in 1841 the *New York Herald Tribune* printed its first issue; and in 1848 Kit Carson carried the first ocean-to-ocean mail from California to the East.

The year 1861 witnessed the attack upon Ft. Sumter; in 1862 slavery was abolished in the District of Columbia; in 1865 Abraham Lincoln was assassinated; that same year General Lee surrendered to General Grant; in 1872 the first formal celebration of Arbor Day took place; in 1881 Jesse James died; 1896 saw the first showing of a motion picture; in 1909 Robert Peary reached the North Pole; in 1912 the *Titanic* sank; in 1927 there was the first public demonstration of long distance television; 1942 was the year when Bataan fell; in 1945 Germany signed an unconditional surrender pact; in 1945 the U.N. was founded; and in 1959 the St. Lawrence Seaway was opened.

In the United States the month of April has seen the beginnings of several wars: April 19, 1775 records the Battles of Lexington and Concord—the start of our fight for independence from England. April 24, 1812, the British burned our national capital. Fort Sumter was fired upon April 14, 1861; in 1898, the United States ordered Spain to leave Cuba, marking the start of the Spanish-American War. Years later, on April 6, 1917, Congress declared war on Germany, and so, the United States entered World War I.

For centuries, the first day of April has been observed as "April Fools' Day" or "All Fools' Day," prompting one early poet to write:

> The first of April some do say
> Is set apart for All Fools' day . . .
> But on this day are people sent
> On purpose for pure merriment.

In various lands the old custom of dispatching persons on fruitless errands has long been practiced. Some sources say this idea stemmed from the travesty of sending Christ (at the time of His trial) from Annas to Caiaphas, and from Pilate to Herod. During the Middle Ages a miracle play was staged at Easter with this pilgrimage as the theme.

In Scotland this was called "hunting the gowk" (cuckoo). In France a person who was fooled in this way was dubbed a *poisson d' Avril* (April fish).

April is an important month for religious festivals as Easter often falls within it, with its special days such as Maundy Thursday, and

Good Friday. The Jewish Passover frequently coincides with Easter; and St. George's Day (patron saint of Great Britain) is noted in April.

Pan American Day—April 14—is celebrated by the American Republics and has for its purpose: "A commemorative symbol of the American Nations and the voluntary union of all in a system known today as the Organization of American States." It is sponsored by the Pan American Union in Washington, D.C.

Nebraska celebrates Arbor Day on April 22, the birthday of J. Sterling Morton, the "Father of Arbor Day." Other states also observe such a day in April, while still others note the holiday at times suited to their climatic conditions.

Patriots' Day (April 19) is especially celebrated in New England. Some Southern states observe their Memorial Days during this month; and down under, Australians and New Zealanders honor their war dead on Anzac Day, April 25.

Thus, our fourth month is an important and much loved one. The Bard of Avon mentioned it several times;

> When well-appointed April on the heel
> Of hurrying winter treads . . .
> —ROMEO AND JULIET

> The April's in her eyes; it is love's spring,
> And these the showers to bring it on.
> —ANTONY AND CLEOPATRA

And in one of his sonnets, Shakespeare wrote:

> From you I have been absent in the spring,
> When proud-pied April dressed in all his trim,
> Hath put a spirit of youth in everything.

John Clare, in his *Shepherd's Calendar* said:

> To see thee smile, all hearts rejoice;
> And warm with feelings strong,
> With thee all nature finds a voice,
> And hums a waking song.

> The lover views thy welcome hours,
> And thinks of summer come,
> And takes the maid thy early flowers
> To tempt her steps from home.

And who can forget those famous lines that Robert Browning wrote of this month when he and his wife Elizabeth Barrett Browning, were living far from their home in Italy:

> Oh, to be in England
> Now that April's there . . .

A modern poet, Jane Merchant, in her poem, "To live with April" declares that the month "is casual with miracles." John Mistletoe states in one poem:

> April prepares her green traffic light
> And the world thinks "Go!"

And most will agree with the delightful description which Enola Chamberlain has penned about this month:

> "No time is lovelier!" I cry
> When springtime rides the April sky.
> When dogwood looks like fallen cloud
> And every robin sings aloud.

April Birthstone—Diamond

The diamond is no doubt the best known of all precious gems and is highly prized for its distinctive beauty.

The name, "diamond," is corrupted from *adamas*, meaning "steel." This stone is the hardest one known; therefore it is widely used not only for jewelry, but for industrial purposes. Usually only the pure white or blue ones, which command the highest prices, are desired for jewelry.

However, according to one source, there are colored diamonds whose "brilliant hues make them among the most striking of gems." They are known in the trade as "fancies," and their shades include golden, yellow, chartreuse, light brown, sapphire blue, brown, pink, rose, brownish pink, black, green, and orchid. Some people believe that the pure white gems are not so spectacular as other more colorful ones, such as emeralds or rubies. It is hard to realize that, after all, a diamond is merely a piece of carbon. However, one authority states that, "to obtain a rough stone which can be cut and polished into a one-carat gem, miners must blast, dig, crush, wash, and sort over 250 tons of ore."

Longer ago than we can imagine—some authorities say over 60,000,000 years—a mass of basic igneous rock (that happened to be free from quartz) was changed by an underground chemical solution into a mineral of bluish-green hue. Tiny carbon particles in the mixture became crystals after exposure to extreme heat and pressure. Then volcanic gases forced the mass to the earth's surface. This crystallized carbon, after cooling, was picked up by rain or stream. Now these choice bits adorn monarchs' crowns, engagement rings, bracelets, watches, and other pieces of jewelry.

The oldest diamonds are known to date from the third century A.D.; they were "natural uncut crystals, not in the least attractive." The first specimens came from gravels in India; later others were discovered in Brazil, South Africa, the Belgian Congo, Sierra Leone, and Tanganyika. For centuries these gems have been highly esteemed; and in ancient times were carried from India and Ceylon, along with other jewels, in camel caravans to be sold in the markets of Europe.

Today, most of the world's supply of diamonds comes from Africa, India, and Brazil. In the last-named country, the gems were first found in 1725, and the mines there have been worked ever since that date. Although Brazil produces only about 5 per cent of the world's output, it has given us some especially fine specimens including the "Southern Star," "Minas Star," "Petrochino," and the "Dresden." As far as value is concerned, the Union of South Africa is the greatest diamond-producing region in the world.

During the 1950's and the year 1960, the Russians began to develop rich diamond mines in the Yakut district of Siberia, on the Lena River at a latitude similar to that of Dawson City and Fairbanks, Alaska. Here Russia now plans to build "hydroelectric dams, roads, industries, and living quarters for the miners and their families." Many new settlers have been taken there to work these new mines; collective farms have been started; and a pioneer camp of 10,000 persons established.

By 1965 the Russians said the district would triple its population, and that they would have a dressing plant with a production capacity of many hundreds of tons of blue ground (the diamond-bearing abrasive) a day. They believe that within a few years, they can produce 9,000,000 carats—half of the present world supply! They plan to use most of the stones in their own industries, and sell the rest on the world markets.

In the United States, a one-carat diamond was once discovered in the state of South Carolina. Other gems have been unearthed in Arkansas, California, Texas, Ohio, Montana, Wisconsin, Kentucky, Idaho, and Virginia. Scientists believe these diamonds were washed there during the Ice Age. Most of the stones found in our country are small and are used in industry.

There is just one locality in the United States where diamonds have been found in their natural matrix, the pipe of a prehistoric volcano. This mine, owned by Mr. Howard Miller, is near Murfreesboro, Arkansas. Every day from 7 A.M. til 6 P.M. visitors may roam over 32 of the 72-acre sector to hunt for the gems. Adults are charged a small fee; children under twelve are allowed to go in free.

It is estimated that an average of about one hundred persons visit the mine daily, with many more on Sundays and holidays. Up to fifty diamonds a month are taken away by visitors. One woman discovered a stone weighing over fifteen carats, valued at $15,000. The Governor of the State named it the "Star of Arkansas." Visitors are permitted to keep what gems they find, however, on those weighing more than five carats, Mr. Miller reserves the right to collect 25 per cent.

This mine has yielded more than 150,000 stones, worth over a million dollars. The largest one ever found here or anywhere in the

United States weighed over 40 carats, and more than 12 when cut and polished. Experts have declared that these Arkansas diamonds are harder for industrial purposes than those from other places and are equal to, if not better, for use as jewelry. However, someone has observed that this mine has not yet been successfully exploited.

In connection with the matter of finding diamonds in the United States, there is the fantastic story of the great diamond hoax that took place in the early 1870's.

Before the scheme was exposed as a terrific fraud, "the cleverly conceived and executed 'salting down' operation" is said to have netted the two sponsors of the nefarious scheme at least $600,000 from an investment of not more than $35,000.

And the strangest thing about this unbelievable affair was that many of America's most astute financial and commercial personalities were so easily taken in by the sharp manipulators. In addition, some of the world's chief authorities on precious jewels unwittingly contributed to the success of this fabulous hoax.

One day two men, named Philip Arnold and John Slack, went to William C. Ralston, a banker and one of the top financiers of the business world in San Francisco. They had two bags containing a collection of jewels, including diamonds, rubies, emeralds, and sapphires. They said they had found them somewhere in the desert and the wily pair declared these were merely a sampling of the millions of dollars' worth of precious stones waiting for discovery.

At once Ralston and other businessmen of San Francisco joined with the Rothschilds of London to exploit this miraculous find. Samples of the gems were inspected in New York by the famous jeweler Tiffany in the presence of Horace Greeley, General George B. McClellan of Civil War fame, and others. Within two days Mr. Tiffany submitted a report that the samples were worth at least $150,000. A company was formed, and Slack and Arnold were paid over $600,000.

Before they got into operation, the U.S. government sent geologist Clarence King to Wyoming to examine the location and make a report. Then to the great chagrin of all concerned, this official soon found that the claim was a fake, that it had been cleverly "salted."

Slack and Arnold had placed gems in crevices of rocks, in artificial ant hills, even in the forks of trees; but not a single stone was ever found there in bedrock. The geologist also pointed out to them that diamonds, rubies, sapphires, and emeralds NEVER were found in the same bed.

So this frenzy of speculation collapsed with a thud. Banker Ralston had to repay $2,000,000 already invested. When Arnold was found in New York, he was forced to give up $150,000, but it is said that he still had $300,000. Later he opened a bank. Slack disappeared and was never heard of again.

And so ended an unbelievable saga—one of the most "exotic episodes in Western history."

Today most of the diamonds produced in the world—totaling about five tons—are not used merely for show and ornaments. They also play an important part in the industrial field for they are vital in the making of fine wire, in turning machine parts, in "trueing" grinding wheels, in drilling for oil, polishing piston rings, in giving long life to phonograph needles, etc. As heat and friction do not affect diamonds, engineers employ them in drilling through rocks; and dentists use them in drilling teeth and in polishing dental fillings.

The price of diamonds is maintained—no matter how many are mined—by a group of Belgian and British interests that control 90 per cent of the world's output; so they manage to keep the market stable. It makes little difference where one buys a diamond; the same size and quality bring a similar price. Headquarters for the diamond industry is located in Hatton Garden, a back street in London. Here, once a month, packages of the stones, termed "sights," are offered to accredited agents.

The centers of the diamond-cutting trade are located in Belgium, where ten to thirteen thousand people are employed; in New York, where much of the South African output is cut; in Palestine, Brazil, Holland, France, South Africa, and the United Kingdom.

In spite of the high price of diamonds, more of these gems are wanted each year. In a recent survey, it was found that 80 per cent of American women under thirty years of age wear diamond engagement rings.

It is interesting to note how styles in such rings have changed. About a century ago, the clustered setting (several small stones banded together and mounted in gold) was the favorite. Then at the turn of the century, solitaires, set high, became the fashion.

Today a modern engagement ring often has a central gem with smaller ones on each side. A diamond really looks whiter when set in platinum; but many persons still prefer yellow gold "as sweet and sentimental," and better suited to go with the traditional plain gold wedding band. Lately some women have been choosing a ring, set with small diamonds, which combines engagement and wedding ring. But some authorities maintain that the single solitaire with matching wedding band remains the most favored.

Originally, a diamond was weighed by balancing it with seeds from the carob tree. However, in 1913, the United States and other countries began to use a standard measure—the metric carat, of which there are 142 (metric carats) to the ounce. Each carat is divided into 100 points, with half a carat equal to 50 points, etc. Statistics show that the average size of the stone in an engagement ring nowadays is 41 points; also that persons living in New York, California, Oklahoma, and Chicago demand the largest gems. As to price, one source says that a full carat stone costs between $450 and $1,680 and half a carat from $150 to $575.

Although the weight of the diamond is important in determining the price, three other factors (the "Three C's")—color, clarity, and cut—are taken into consideration. Most highly prized are the colorless or blue-white stones, but few have the deep pure color that gives them "superlative rating."

"Clarity," according to expert Larry Smith, "refers to the presence—or absence—of flaws or inclusions in a diamond. . . . Many of them are not visible to the naked eye."

The American Gem Society recommends to its trained jewelers

definite terms to describe degree of clarity: flawless, very slightly imperfect, slightly imperfect, and imperfect.

Many believe that the beauty of the stone is due to the skill of the cutter. It is only in modern times that man evolved the correct geometric pattern of cutting to reveal the gem's greatest beauty. The round or brilliant cut has 58 facets, and its "fire" depends upon the lights reflected from them.

For ages diamonds have been the choice of members of the royalty and nobility, and such stones have played important roles in history. At the height of her glory, Marie Antoinette adorned herself with various pieces of jewelry, glittering with fine diamonds. Queen Victoria especially prized a ring in the shape of a snake which had a diamond set in each of its twelve joints. This had been given to her by Prince Albert.

The mother of Queen Elizabeth II often wears diamond clips shaped like a feather or plume with her costumes. And her daughter enjoys using diamond brooches in the shape of a Rhodesian lily or a maple leaf, while for formal affairs she wears pear-shaped diamond earrings of the chandelier type.

René Lecler recently said that Queen Elizabeth is "never hard up for a trinket to wear," and that last Christmas when she went shopping, "the brooch she wore on her town suit was made up of diamonds once a part of the famous Cullinan stone."

She has a fabulous collection that is kept in a safe in Buckingham Palace. Her husband, Prince Philip, has made a complete catalogue of the royal jewels. One of the Queen's favorites is what she calls "Granny's Tiara," bequeathed to her by her grandmother, the late Queen Mary. At the front it is eighteen inches high and is set with 178 diamonds.

Another of her tiaras is a magnificent diamond piece with nineteen superb hanging drop pearls. Her wedding presents included a three-tiered rose diamond tiara from the Nizam of Hyderabad. From her noted ancestor Queen Victoria, Queen Elizabeth received a necklace whose center piece is a 24-carat diamond. Another outstanding gem in her collection is a pink diamond—three quarters of an inch in diameter—from East Africa.

Through past centuries, several exceptionally large stones have been mined, and various interesting stories are connected with them. For example, in 1905 Frederick Wells, surface manager of a mine in South Africa, found the "Cullinan," weighing 3,106 carats—about one and a third pounds, the largest one ever discovered.

The Transvaal Government bought this stone, and presented it to King Edward VII on his sixty-sixth birthday. Later the diamond was divided into five sections, four of which were placed in the Crown Jewels. One, a pear-shaped gem, "the Great Star of Africa," is mounted in the sceptre, and is said to be the largest in the world.

Another noted diamond, the "Kohinoor" (also British property), weighed 109 carats. A legend regarding it was that its possessor would rule the world. There are some missing links in its history, but one source believes it *may* have been the Orloff diamond that once belonged to Catherine the Great.

For many years this gem passed by inheritance through a long line of Mogul emperors, until stolen in 1739 by Nadir, Shah of Persia. Several rulers suffered misfortunes while this stone was in their hands. Finally the British gained possession of it when they annexed the Punjab. From this diamond 80 carats were cut and in 1911 the main section was placed in Queen Mary's crown.

Another diamond, the "Regent," 410 carats uncut, was concealed in the wooden leg of an Indian servant who had discovered it. Then an English sea captain stole the gem from the Indian and threw the native into the ocean. Later, filled with remorse for his misdeed, the officer committed suicide.

An ancestor of William Pitt bought the Regent for $100,000. It was cut to 143.2 carats and became the property of the French Regent. Napoleon pawned it in Holland for money to carry on the Battle of Marengo, and when he was crowned the gem was set in his sword.

Several wealthy Americans (among them the noted art collector, Mrs. Jack Gardner) have owned distinctive diamonds. The most talked about jewels in Boston were two large stones which she called the "Light of India" and the "Rajah." The owner often wore these handsome gems on gold springs in her hair; and as she walked, they "glimmered like antennae."

On her travels in the Orient Mrs. Gardner was received by the King of Cambodia. On this important occasion, she wore the two white diamonds in the strings of her black lace bonnet. And on the front of her dress was her equally famous yellow diamond.

After Fenway Court was completed, the mistress of this outstanding gallery often had concerts there with notable singers participating. When Madame Nellie Melba, the well known prima donna, gave a program in the Dutch Room, Mrs. Gardner afterwards presented the costly yellow diamond to the diva. She declared that, although the King of Cambodia had wanted it, she had saved it for the "Queen of Song."

That fabulous stone weighing 44.5 carats, the renowned "Hope" diamond, has no doubt received more publicity than any other. This rare blue stone, once the property of Louis XIV, was purchased in 1909, in Paris, by Edward B. McLean, whose wife, Evalyn Walsh McLean, used it as a pendant on a chain. She loved to share it with others and wore it constantly, even to ball games. When Mrs. McLean visited veterans' hospitals, she would take it off, and let the men handle it.

The story goes that centuries ago a Brahman priest stole it from a Burmese temple idol, and he was tortured to death for his crime. Then, during the 1660's, Jean Baptiste Tavernier bought the stone in India, and in 1686 sold it to Louis XIV. Tavernier's dissolute son squandered the money it brought, and the father met a tragic death.

After the diamond had been cut down, as part of the French crown jewels, it was called the "French Blue." From then on a long line of misfortunes came to all who had any connection with it. Nicholas Fouquet was executed; Princess de Lamballe was beaten to death by a French mob; King Louis XVI and his Queen, Marie Antoinette, who inherited it, were beheaded.

During the French Revolution the stone disappeared. After several decades (during which it was chipped down to its present weight) it turned up in London. There, in 1830, it was sold to Henry Hope for $90,000. From this time it was called the "Hope" diamond. The "curse"—so the story goes—struck his grandson, and the latter's wife, May Yohe, an American actress, was reduced to scrubbing floors.

In 1867 the Hope diamond was sold at an auction in London for $400,000, and reached the hands of Sultan Abdullah Hamid of Turkey. He lost his throne in 1890; and his wife—wearer of the famous jewel—and child were killed by a fall from a cliff.

After the McLeans had purchased the Hope diamond, the first son lost his life in an accident; the husband was involved in the Teapot Dome scandal and died in a mental hospital. A daughter succumbed from an overdose of sleeping tablets; and Mrs. McLean was said to have become addicted to morphine. Before her death she is supposed to have refused $2,000,000 for the stone.

Two years later, Harry Winston, a New York dealer, bought the noted diamond, exhibited it all over the world, and raised huge sums for charity, declaring he had had more than his money out of it. In November, 1958, Mr. Winston presented the Hope diamond to the Smithsonian Institution, in Washington, D.C., and seems to have escaped the misfortunes of so many past owners of the gem.

After the diamond was safely delivered to the Smithsonian, a newspaper story told of several pieces of bad luck that had happened to the postman, James G. Todd, who had carried the stone to the Institution. And, since the government now owns the Hope diamond, Mr. Todd gave this word of warning: if the hex is supposed to affect the owners, then the American public should be having a run of bad luck.

At a Christmas party at the Smithsonian Institution in 1965, Harry Winston's son called the affair, given to honor the opening of the new Jade Hall, the "Rock Garden." Guests that evening were seated near the noted Hope diamond. (The Director announced that the Smithsonian is looking for someone with two million dollars to purchase the third largest diamond in the world, the "Jubilee," weighing 263 carats. It is in Switzerland, awaiting a buyer.)

In 1960 a collection of diamonds made news when it was sold at auction in New York. The gems, 158 pieces, had been owned by Mrs. Lillian G. Timken, and sold for the large sum of $1,695, 470. This sale was attended by more than 1200 prospective buyers, from all parts of the globe. One gem of 28.75 carats, set in a ring, brought $157,500, a world's record.

The proceeds of this sale went to various charities, including the American Red Cross, Boy Scouts, Community Service Society of New York, Memorial Hospital for the Treatment of Cancer and Allied Diseases, the New York Association for the Blind, and the Travelers' Aid Society of New York.

Also in 1960, in London, what is said to have been the largest diamond ever offered at a public auction, was withdrawn when the bidding stopped at 65,000 pounds as this was less than the price the owners had set. This gem was believed to have been the property of ex-Queen Geraldine of Albania, then living at Cannes. (In 1939, when she and her husband fled Albania at the time of the Italian occupation, it was reported that they took with them five million dollars' worth of jewels.) A second diamond, unmounted and uncut, was bid up to 13,000 pounds and this too was withdrawn from the sale.

In December, 1964, a big blue and white diamond weighing 30.58 carats sold at Sotheby's auction rooms in London for 70,000 pounds —a record price for an unmounted diamond.

This stone, oblong in shape, with cut corners, was said to have been part of the collection owned by Cardinal Mazarin, first minister to King Louis XIV of France. A woman, whose identity was kept secret, sent it from Switzerland to be sold. Before the sale, a spokesman for Sotheby's declared: "This is a marvelous stone, a real beauty."

Recently Barbara Hutton purchased for an unknown sum a diamond weighing 48 carats. She has named it the "Champassak Diamond" in honor of her seventh husband, Prince Doan Vink de Champassak.

Top jewelry designers compete each year in the Diamonds—International Awards for imaginative design in precious jewelry. In

1963, a young British free-lance designer, Gilian Packard, was awarded one of the twenty-four prizes for her "fireworks" brooch, which Miss Packard described as "a sunburst of topaz crystals, with pink and yellow gold and baguette diamonds scattered in the center."

Through the years since they were first discovered, various superstitions have grown up around these priceless stones. For instance, some ancient peoples believed that a diamond could ward off evil from its possessor, heal his diseases, or attract good fortune to him. A diamond was frequently worn as a talisman to keep a warrior safe in battle. King John of France, for instance, was wearing a diamond when captured by Edward of England, the Black Prince, at Poitiers in 1356.

An old Hindu legend predicted death for the owner of a red-spotted stone. Another interesting belief was that snakes could produce gems, including diamonds. Some also thought that two diamonds, if watered with dew, would yield smaller stones of their kind.

Because of their great value, all down through the years, diamonds have been stolen by clever thieves. Many of them have never been recovered. In the past four years—up to 1966—several such robberies have occurred in the so-called "Diamond Belt" in the northern part of Dallas, Texas.

These repeated feats have been successfully carried out by the noted "King of Diamonds," who is said to have stolen more than a million dollars' worth of the precious gems in this region.

His trademarks are "selectivity" and "waffle-shaped footprints." The "King" takes only the finest of diamonds and jewelry. After his latest robbery—early in January, 1966—a satin bag with less costly jewels was found, discarded, under a hedge.

These distinctive gems have often been mentioned in literary works, and have played important roles in several pieces of fiction. Cervantes, the author of *Don Quixote*, once asserted: "Every tooth in a man's head is more valuable than a diamond."

And it was Joris K. Huysmans who made this derogatory statement: "The diamond has become notoriously common, since every tradesman has taken to wearing it on his little finger."

In spite of this last remark, the April birthstone is still most highly prized all over the world, for as one unknown source has well said: "A diamond is a thing apart. The most precious of gems, costliest of jewels. A diamond is symbolic of many things . . . associated with life's happier moments."

April Flower—Sweet Pea

> Here are sweet peas on tip-toe for flight,
> With wings of gentle flush o'er delicate white.
> —JOHN KEATS

This young English poet delighted in the sweet pea, the April flower. For many years it has also been a favorite of gardeners and flower lovers in general, because of its fragrance, beauty, and ease of cultivation.

The name comes from the Latin, *pisum*, which became "pyse" in medieval English, and finally "peas." The sweet pea is said to have descended from an annual, "a weedy little plant" that grew wild on the islands of Sicily, Sardinia, and in southern Italy, reaching England about 1700.

Our modern varieties are quite different from the old fashioned kinds of centuries ago, which were reported as having "blue wings and purple standards." Some types have lost much of the beautiful odor of the early ones. One source states that the pure white and purple sweet peas are natives of lands around the Mediterranean, while the red ones originated in Ceylon.

This flower is a hardy annual climbing plant, with rough stems, long stalks, tendril-bearing leaves, and seed pods, one to two inches long. The blossom—which may be two inches across—has five petals; the upper one is larger than the others, and "encloses them in a pod." Some have plain petals, while others are fringed or wavy. Sweet peas come in both double and "hooded" types and are distinguished by different hues: white, delicate shades of pink and lavender, red, blue, and purple; in fact, they may be almost any color except yellow.

They are grown both out of doors and in greenhouses. There are hundreds of varieties; some are dwarfs, while others, if supported on trellises, may grow to heights of six or seven feet. The perennial, or "everlasting sweet pea," bears clusters of flowers in different sizes and varied hues. This kind is popular because of its handsome, but scentless flowers. There is an old belief that if you plant sweet peas on Good Friday, or on St. Patrick's day, they will grow more abundantly.

The first known history of this flower begins about 1650. According to one authority, in 1699, a devout monk and enthusiastic botanist, Father Franciscus Cupini, sent from his garden in Palermo, Italy, some seeds of small red and blue sweet peas to Dr. Uvedale, master of a school near Enfield, England. This teacher was noted as a curious collector and introducer of many rare and exotic plants and flowers. Holland also obtained sweet peas about the same time that Britain did.

By 1760, the seeds were on sale in the British Isles and "sweet scented peas" were being sold on London streets. Several new types were created and marketed, among them the "Painted Lady," and the "Blanche Ferry." Colonel Trevor Clarke of Daventry experimented with sweet peas and produced white ones with blue edges.

English botanists were enthusiastic about these flowers; for a time they seemed more interested than growers did. Finally, about the middle of the 19th century, the latter took their development more seriously.

In 1876, when there were only a dozen kinds on the market, Henry Eckford began his important work of developing sweet peas, and because of his great and abiding interest, these blooms grew to the number and in the color, form, and variety we enjoy today.

At the 1900 Bicentennial Show at the Crystal Palace in London, 264 different kinds of sweet peas were exhibited, with wonderful improvements in shape and hue; some also had four blossoms on each stem, instead of the usual two. Of the 264 varieties, 115 had originated at Henry Eckford's nursery at Wem in Shropshire.

Once, *The Daily Mail* offered a prize for the best bowl of sweet peas. This was won by Silas Cole, who originated and distributed a new variety, "with waved and frilled flowers, increased size, and attractive color." Cole had developed this plant from Eckford's "Prima Donna," and he named it the "Countess Spencer" to honor the wife of his employer. It had big, wide flowers, but not so much fragrance as some earlier sweet peas.

Thus, for many decades these blossoms have been popular with both amateur and commercial gardeners in the British Isles. During the Edwardian era they were especially popular as table decorations. They were also the favorite flowers of Queen Alexandra, wife of Edward VII.

Before the opening of the twentieth century, the greater amount of sweet pea seeds was produced in England. Since then, these plants have been grown in great quantities in the United States, particularly in California where the climate is ideal for producing such seeds. Since 1900, about 100,000 pounds—most of the world's supply—have been grown annually in this country, with a fifth of the output coming from one company in the state of California.

Alternate April Flower—Daisy

> Daisies, ye flowers of lowly birth
> Embroideries of the carpet birth,
> That stud the velvet sod;
> Open to spring's refreshing air,
> In sweetest smiling bloom declare
> Your maker and my God.

The alternate flower for April, the daisy—popular name of flowering herbs of the family Carduacae—is one of the oldest and best known of English flowers. It still retains its Anglo-Saxon name, "the day's eye," appropriately given to it because of its appearance and the fact that its petals close at night.

A favorite in Scotland, there it is called "gowan" or "measure of love"; and in England, "herb Margaret." Other names attached to it include "star of the earth" and "companion of the sun." In France, the daisy is "la belle marguerite," which means "pearl," and refers to the whiteness of its petals. In Wales it has been termed the "trembling star."

An English writer, of the past century, William Hone, said that the daisy "usually graced the meadows about February 22, the festival day of St. Margaret of Cortona."

Daisies have been admired by young and old for many centuries. Children love to roam through fields of them, and to make chains of the blossoms. Garlands of daisies have for years been used by colleges and other schools in their graduation exercises.

The common white daisy was introduced in America at an early date. "Conquering our territory," it multiplied fast. This white daisy is found in Canada and in our northeastern states, but is not so common in the south and west. This ordinary field flower—often called the oxeye daisy—is a rather tall plant, with slender, erect stems—stiff and soldierly—as someone has described it. Its head is a bright yellow disk, and the white rays measure from one to two inches across. This kind blooms from May to November in open, sunny fields and meadows.

There is another common wild flower of the daisy family in our country called "Black-eyed Susan," "Golden Jerusalem," or simply, "Yellow Daisy." Usually it is a biennial, but sometimes an annual, with heavy, rough stems and leaves. The flower heads are showy, with yellow rays, and a brown, black, or purple cone-shaped center.

This kind of daisy is a native of the plains and western prairies; but now it is also well established in our eastern region from Quebec southward to Florida, and westward to Colorado and Texas, as well as along the Pacific Coast. Black-eyed Susans bloom from July to September, often in rich soil along the banks of streams. It frequently grows so abundantly in meadows and pastures that farmers consider it an obnoxious weed, and many cattle avoid it.

There are other varieties of daisies including the Michaelmas daisy, a term applied to American asters. (Some wild asters are also referred to as daisies.) On high ranges as far west as Colorado, can be found mountain daisies, with violet or purple rays.

Several types are cultivated in gardens, in various shades of red, pink, and white. A popular double daisy with a golden center has been named the "Shasta Daisy," a beautiful and very sturdy blossom. This famous hybrid was developed by the well-known horticulturist, Luther Burbank, who named it for snowcapped Mt. Shasta in northern California. This has large white flowers, about four inches in diameter, with a stem from one to two feet high. It often blooms all summer and is prized for its beauty.

One popular plant called "African daisy" grows in many gardens. It stems from ancestors in sub-tropical South Africa; and during the years, several hybrids have been developed from it. These are bushy, have woolly white foliage, and sometimes grow to a height of thirty inches. The blossoms vary in color from silvery white with blue, through shades of yellow, light orange, and rust. The petals are grouped around a darkly colored center.

When Americans think of daisies, a picture of the ordinary white flower usually comes to mind. However, the "daisy proper"—so often extolled by poets in classical English literature—is, in fact, the English daisy, "Bellis perennis" which someone has said, "hugs the English turf."

The term "Bellis" is derived from *Belides*, the Greek name for dryads (nymphs supposed to reside in trees). One of these graceful beings, it has been said, was seen dancing on the green by the god of spring, Vertumnus. At once he tried to clasp her in his arms; but she was transformed, and "sank to the earth in the form of a little daisy."

Such daisies, native to Europe, grew plentifully there, and often completely covered fields and pastures, and inspired many poets. One, James E. Flexner, wrote these lines:

> Meadows of England, shining in the rain,
> Spread out your daisied lawns.

Long ago, Shakespeare, who mentioned many different flowers in his dramas and sonnets, expressed his feelings for these blooms in such words:

> When daisies pied and violets blue . . .
> Do paint the meadows with delight.

John Milton, too, spoke of "meadows trim with daisies pied," (the last old-fashioned word means "parti-colored"). Wordsworth, in *To the Daisy* declared:

> A nun demure, of lovely port;
> Or sprightly maiden of Love's Court . . .
> I see thee glittering from afar,
> And then thou art a pretty star.

Chaucer loved this blossom—"the daisie, or else the eie of the day"—which each evening shuts its rays and opens them again the next day. Chaucer was probably the first person to discover this fact. He once described a green valley "with daisies powdered over." Often he rose early and went out to see them open; and that same evening he watched the flowers "go to sleep," inspiring him to write:

> To see this flower, how it will go to rest,
> For fear of the night, so hateth it the darkness.

This English daisy having a head with a yellow disk, surrounded by small white or pink rays, really belongs to the aster family. One species of Bellis perennis is found in the United States, confined chiefly to Kentucky, Tennessee, Arkansas, and some southwestern states.

The English daisy reached our continent many years ago. One source says it was "a stowaway in the hay, brought to the United States to feed the horses in General Burgoyne's army." This plant has often "run away" from its original place of growth, and stars grassy lawns with its small delicately hued rays. According to one writer:

It is such a wanderer that it must have been one of the first flowers that strayed outside the Garden of Eden.

Often the daisy has been used to "prognosticate," especially in matters of love, following the famous example of Marguerite in *Faust*, who plucked off the petals while murmuring "He loves me; he loves me not." In her poem, *The Sign of the Daisy*, Helen Hunt Jackson wrote of this:

> All summer she scattered the daisy leaves,
> They only mocked her as they fell.
> She said, "The daisy but deceives;
> There is no virtue in its spell.
> "He loves me not," "He loves me well,"
> One story no two daisies tell.

And an old popular song contains this chorus:

> Daisy, Daisy, give me your answer, do,
> I'm half crazy, all for the love of you . . .

Several superstitions became associated with these blossoms; for instance, an English milkmaid would put roots of this plant under her pillow to help her dream of her lover. In the spring, one was supposed to step on the first daisy he saw if he did not want such blossoms to grow on his own grave, or that of a dear one, before the year was over. And the spirits of babies that died at birth were said to scatter flowers on earth to cheer their saddened parents. An old Celtic legend mentioned daisies in this connection:

The flowers in primitive times were used as magic charms to cure wounds, gouts, fevers; to remove warts; to change gray hair to black; and as an ointment to clear the eye. A patient afflicted with insanity was forced to drink a potion made from ingredients including daisies for fifteen days.

For many centuries the daisy has been featured in heraldries and was quite popular as an emblem in coats of arms or engraved on signet rings. Pearls in the shape of daisies were sometimes set in gold.

Few blossoms have so long been famed in history, legend, and poetry as daisies. They have been associated with several queens named Margaret or Marguerite. For example, Marguerite of Anjou showed her preference for this flower when she wore three daisies at her wedding to Henry VI of England. When she was welcomed at the English court, she saw these blooms embroidered on the robes and cloaks of the British nobility in her honor. The attendants' garb was likewise decorated with daisies.

It is said that the Order of the Daisy was started in France to honor Marguerite of Flanders, sister of Francis I. Marguerite of Valois married Henry of Navarre in 1572. A few years later she visited Bordeaux, and at a reception received a bouquet of marguerites. She assured the people that they would be her special flower. At the ancient castle of Usson, this queen had a garden with many daisies in it. After her divorce from the king, she made her home in Paris, and at Issy created a famous garden in which "Paris daisies" were cultivated. Later this estate became a monastery.

Lady Margaret Beaufort, mother of Henry VII, used the daisy as her badge, or emblem. When the king built his beautiful chapel at Westminster Abbey between 1485 and 1509, his mother's badge of three daisies was sculptured among its ornaments.

This modest flower also honors one of the six saints named Margaret, the daughter of a heathen priest at Antioch. She was driven from her home because she would not give up her Christian faith. Later she was known as St. Margaret of the Dragon.

St. Louis wore a ring on which were engraved a crucifix, a fleur-de-lis, and a daisy, representing all he held most dear—religion, France, and his wife.

William C. Bennett once called the daisy, "the smile of God"; and the poet, James Montgomery wrote of it:

> There is a flower, a little flower,
> With silver crest and golden eye,
> That welcomes every changing hour
> And weathers every day . . .
> The rose has but a summer reign,
> The daisy never dies.

Apparently, James Montgomery was right in his statement that "the daisy never dies." Even though it's a far cry from the time when Chaucer went out to see this flower open and close, the simple daisy is still much loved today. Recently it was honored in an unusual and modern way when, during January, 1966, a unique art show was put on at the Setay Gallery in Beverly Hills, California.

The show, cleverly named "If You Dig Daisies," was the third one-subject display arranged by Diane Rosner. It took her more than a year to prepare the show which included 135 paintings, sculptures, etc. Almost fifty artists entered works in oils, water-colors, charcoal, ink, metals, pottery, and sculpture. These exhibits came from artists in California, Colorado, New York, Spain, Belgium, Germany, and Italy.

It was really amazing to note the varied and unusual fashions in which the artists featured these simple flowers. There were land-scapes, seascapes, and still-life scenes. Seed pods along with full blooms were shown, both in white and yellow types. Tiny flowers as well as the large showy Shasta daisies were pictured. Sometimes a flower was alone, but often daisies were combined in intriguing ways with other elements.

Daisies were arranged in various kinds of receptacles including unusual bottles, vases, baskets, and pitchers. One group in a bowl had a vivid yellow-orange background; children were holding daisies; a cat had one in its paw; while another daisy was perched jauntily on a dog's head. One striking painting was that of a gondola carrying a lion with a halo of yellow daisy petals.

Some pictures showed large masses of flowers: one, in front of an old home; in another a bunch of white daisies stood out with a brilliant blue background, while in another, a hand clasped a spray of the flowers. There were paintings in which but a lone daisy was seen in a field or desert. One striking work was a large daisy boldly staring through some fence palings.

Sometimes people were seen in action: two nuns in black robes were picking the flowers in a field; at a carousel there was a lady with a black hat wreathed with daisies; a sleeping tramp—executed in pottery—was clasping one flower in his hand.

Several young girls held or wore daisies; one a modern young nude, with a high hair-do had a lap full of the flowers. A cleverly contrived wire structure showed a humming bird hovering over a flower. One of the finest pieces displayed came from Germany. It was reverse painting on glass, depicting a mythical character, half man, half daisy. There was a clever bit of humor in a picture captioned "She Loves Me!"; showing a smiling mouse perched on a daisy whose petals he had just plucked.

Altogether this display showed imagination and much ingenuity on the part of the artists, proved that this lowly little flower is still loved. So this enjoyable exhibit was a well deserved tribute to one of the flowers dedicated to our month of April.

May

Then came faire May, the fayrest mayd on ground,
Deckt with all the dainties of her season's pryde,
And throwing flow'res out of her lap around . . .
                                            —EDMUND SPENSER

FROM early eras, our fifth month, "the merry month of May,"
has been associated with dancing, singing, love, and general rejoicing that spring has returned after a long and dreary winter. Shakespeare once said that someone was "as full of spirit as the month of
May," while a modern poet, Louise Moulton, wrote:

> The month it was the month of May . . .
> And all the flowers sprang up to see . . .

An older writer expressed his reaction to May in this fashion:

> . . . And with the heart of May
> Doth every beast keep holiday.

And who can forget Robert Browning's inspiring lines showing
the gladness with which his "wise thrush" greets this happy month:

> And after April, when May follows,
> And the whitethroat builds, and all the swallows . . .
> That's the wise thrush; he sings each song twice over,
> Lest you should think he never could recapture
> The first fine careless rapture!

For some time, May was the third month on the Roman Calendar, and under the protection of the god Apollo. At the beginning, May was given only twenty-two days, then thirty-one, later reduced to thirty, and finally ending with thirty-one.

There are differences of opinion as to how the month got its name. The term *may* come from the name of the goddess, Maia, "brightest of the Pleiades," mother of Mercury, and the deity of "growth and increase." Maia is said to have been the daughter of Atlas, who held up the earth, and a sea nymph. On May Day it was customary for Romans to march in a procession to the grotto of Egena, where they carried out ceremonies honoring the revival of vegetation, and to assure abundant crops.

Other authorities maintain that May was so-named to pay tribute to the Majores (or Maiores), the older branch of the Roman Senate.

On May Day Romans continued their observance of the floral games—the Floralia—which had started late in April. These were dedicated to Flora, goddess of flowers. Everyone gathered boughs and blossoms to adorn her temple and statue, and young men used to hang wreaths and garlands on their sweethearts' homes.

Roman ladies on the first day of this month made offerings to Bona Dea, the "good goddess," or "the earth." She was depicted with a lion, and was accompanied by the signs of the Zodiac "which influence our sphere to produce its fruits in due order."

The Saxons called May "Tri-milchi"; for on May Day they turned their cows out to pasture. Because of the abundance of grass, the milk was of finer quality, the cows yielded much more abundantly, and so had to be milked three times each day. It was in May that dairymen began making cheese.

Since May Day was symbolic of a return to life, of the defeat of the hard winter, with new hopes for good planting and rich harvests, the people, during the time of the Druids, made special sacrifices, even including human beings in these rites. They built great bonfires on hillsides, leaped over the flames, or drove cattle through them. It is said that this custom continued in some parts of Britain as late as the eighteenth century.

In medieval and Tudor England May Day was an important public holiday, with varied festivities and customs. In 1791 one London paper reported:

Yesterday, being the first of May, a number of persons went into the fields and bathed their faces with the dew on the grass, with the idea that it would render them beautiful.

This superstition was widespread in England, and the noted writer, Samuel Pepys, mentioned it in his diary.

On this festive holiday, all classes of people would rise at dawn to go "a-maying." From nearby woods they would return laden with flowers and branches of trees with which they decorated their homes.

One of the most important features of May Day was the choosing and crowning of a May Queen to reign over the games, dancing, and other festivities. These celebrations were held in large cities like London as well as in the small villages. In his well-known poem, Tennyson referred to the custom in these words:

> For I'm to be Queen o' the May, Mother,
> I'm to be Queen of the May.

Maypoles often were set up just for the occasion, however, in some larger places the poles were erected permanently. (In 1661, for instance, one—134 feet tall—was set up in the Strand.) Of course the gay dancing around a maypole was anathema to the strict Puritans. In 1583, John Stubbs spoke of those "stinckyng idols about which the people leape and dance as the heathen did."

When the monarchy was overthrown, the Puritans made many changes. In 1644 Parliament forbade the erection of Maypoles, but with the return of the king to power the poles again became popular.

The celebration of May Day as a time of rejoicing, singing and dancing around Maypoles has continued in the British Isles; it has also become an annual custom in the United States, especially at schools and public playgrounds.

It was during May that the popular and long-anticipated May Fair took place in London, near Piccadilly, and the district around there still retains the name of Mayfair.

Since the weather in May was often unsettled and uncertain, persons were warned against changing into lighter-weight clothing too soon:

> Change not a clout
> Till May is out.

Another old adage went, "A hot May makes a fat churchyard." The month was considered a trying one, especially for individuals afflicted with critical complaints. Often it was said of a person: "Ah, he'll never get up May-hill," or "If he can climb May-hill, he'll do." Here is some advice given by a Doctor Foster:

As a rule of health for May, we may advise early rising, in particular, as being conducive to that blessing. Everything now invites the sluggard to leave his bed and go abroad.

Farmers in some localities believed that May weather influenced their crops, as expressed in this couplet:

> Mist in May and heat in June,
> Make the harvest right soon.

And often in old calendars, May was designated as the month of love:

> Two lovers stray in a forest green . . .
> And there they talk unheard and walk unseen,
> Save by the birds, who chat a louder lay,
> To welcome such true lovers with the May.

A poet named Darwin was inspired to pen these lines:

> Hail, Bounteous May, that doth inspire
> Mirth, and youth and warm desire . . .

Even though the month of May was dedicated to love, some early peoples regarded it as unlucky for marriages, in fact, sometimes weddings were prohibited. May was the time when expiations were made. The Lemuria, the festival of "the unhappy dead," occurred in May. Ovid wrote of the idea that May was not the time for marriage, and the belief still persists in some places today.

May, like some other months, has been praised by writers, one of whom declared that in May

Spring is with us once more, pacing the earth in all the primal pomp of her beauty, with flowers and soft airs and the songs of birds everywhere about her, and the blue sky and the bright clouds above.

John Clare, in his *Shepherd's Calendar*, pays tribute to this month, which is termed "the offspring of the solar beams":

> How lovely now are lanes and balks
> For lovers on their Sunday walks!
> The daisy and the buttercup—
> For which the laughing children stoop
> A hundred times throughout the day,
> In their rude romping summer play—
> So thickly now the pasture crowd
> In a gold and silver sheeted cloud,
> As if the drops of April showers
> Had woo'd the sun and changed to flowers.

Quite in contrast to Clare's lines are the following by the noted New England poet, Amy Lowell, as she describes May in her region:

> May is lilac time here in New England,
> May is a thrush singing "Sun up" in a tip-top ash tree . . .

Two Presidents, Harry S. Truman and John F. Kennedy, were born in May, but this month also contains the birthdays of numerous others who have attained fame in various fields: James J. Audubon, Sigmund Freud, Walt Whitman, Robert Browning, Patrick Henry, Peter the Great of Russia, Dolly Madison, Tschaikowsky, John Brown, Florence Nightingale, Ezio Pinza, Madame Nellie Melba,

Richard Wagner, Queen Victoria, and the great musician, Johannes Brahms.

Others include Bob Hope, the Dionne Quintuplets, Christopher Columbus, Ralph Waldo Emerson, Irving Berlin, Henry Kaiser, Willie Mays, Norman Vincent Peale, and Kate Smith.

During May, down through the centuries, history-making events have occurred. In 1537 Anne Boleyn was beheaded; in 1607 the first permanent settlement was made at Jamestown, Virginia; in 1616 Manhattan Island was purchased for about twenty-four dollars; in 1797 the United States launched its first naval vessel; in 1802 Napoleon established the Legion of Honor and in 1821 his death occurred at St. Helena; in 1823 "Home, Sweet Home" was sung for the first time in London; in 1840 England issued the first postage stamp in the world—the famous "Penny Black."

In 1847 the American Medical Association was formed; in 1862 the U.S. Department of Agriculture was established; the next year, 1863, the first paid fire department was started in New York City; also that year the first Memorial Day was observed; 1869 saw the completion of our first transcontinental railroad; in 1881 the American Red Cross was organized by Clara Barton; in 1898 the Battle of Manila Bay was fought; and in 1907 the first taxi cab in the U.S.A. went into operation.

In 1907 Miss Anna Jarvis started the observance of Mother's Day; in 1915 the *Lusitania* was sunk; in 1917 the Selective Service Act became effective; in 1918 the first regular air mail service was begun, between New York and Washington; in 1922 the Lincoln Memorial in the national capital was dedicated; 1925 witnessed the first transatlantic flight; in 1942 the aircraft carrier, *Lexington*, was sunk, and Corregidor was surrendered; and in 1945 came V-E Day and the surrender of Germany.

As mentioned earlier, the first day in May has long been observed as one of merriment, with people rejoicing over the return of spring. In recent years this date has taken on added significance. For in many American cities "Law Day" is noted on the first of May. Its purpose is "to foster deeper respect for law, encourage responsible citizenship, and emphasize the rule of law versus the rule of force."

In the State of Hawaii "Lei Day" is celebrated May 1. It is the time "for wearing leis and honoring the spirit of the lei, which is friendliness and goodwill." This holiday is sponsored by the city and county of Honolulu.

The first day of our fifth month is also celebrated in many places around the globe to commemorate "the international solidarity of workingmen." In 1889 the International Socialist Congress designated the date as an international labor holiday, to honor labor, just as citizens of the U.S.A. do on Labor Day, the first Monday in September.

Other May holidays include such special days as Mother's Day (the second Sunday in the month); Armed Forces Day (the third Saturday), which replaces former Air Forces, Army, and Navy Days; National Maritime Day falls on May 22, the date of the first crossing of the Atlantic by steam by the little steamer, *Savannah*. This date is set apart by Presidential proclamation to honor the American Merchant Marine.

Victoria Day (or Empire Day), May 24, honors the birthday of the noted British queen. An important religious holiday—Ascension Day—comes during May (40 days after Easter) and commemorates Christ's ascension into Heaven.

Memorial Day (formerly Decoration Day, or Prayer for Peace) is observed on May 30 in the majority of American states to remind citizens of the supreme sacrifice made by so many of our soldiers.

May Birthstone—Emerald

> And ice, mast high, came floating by
> as green as emerald . . .
>   —COLERIDGE

The peerless emerald has always been one of the most desired and expensive of jewels. Pliny ranked it third, and declared: Indeed there is not a stone the color of which is more delightful to the eye.

This gem is composed of silicates of beryllium and aluminum and is said to get its green color from the chromium contained in it. An emerald is highly prized for its distinctive beauty and unlike many gems, does not lose its pure color when viewed in artificial light.

Emeralds are comparatively soft, and very few are found that are absolutely flawless. Often the deepest colored ones have some imperfections. Aside from their use as jewelry, these stones are not adaptable for industry, as are several others. They are popular for rings, and would be used more often in larger pieces if it were not for their high cost. Authorities say it is difficult to quote a price for a natural emerald, for the gems vary in size, color, and quality. One weighing three carats may sell from $600 to $9,000 or more.

According to H. P. Whitlock, the emerald

. . . is today the supreme high point in gem value, having by reason of popular mode, which demands green rather than red stones, outranked even the ruby in this respect.

Good emeralds have been discovered in the Ural Mountains, in Russian territory, on the Asiatic side, in the Austrian Tyrol, India, Ceylon, Madagascar, and Burma. A few small ones have come from North Carolina. Recently some have been found in South Africa. Most sources agree that the finest emeralds come from Colombia in South America, and that the specimens mined in Egypt and Russia cannot compare with them.

There is a legend in Southern California that many years ago the Cahuilla Indians who lived below Palm Springs, near the Borrego Desert worked emerald mines in the Santa Rosa Mountains. It is claimed that these natives brought in many valuable shining green emeralds which they gave to their medicine men who used them to ward off sickness and evil spirits. The location of the mines—so the story goes—was formerly marked by a large rock, shaped like the head of a wolf or coyote. During an earthquake this stone fell into a canyon. Today the old Indian trails to the mines are obliterated, and the location of the lost emerald mines still remains a mystery.

Through the ages, emeralds have often been mentioned in various writings; those of Cleopatra were famous. They probably came from the "Cleopatra" mines in Upper Egypt. These mines were abandoned, then lost and rediscovered in 1818, when the Viceroy of Egypt sent Cailliaud out to search for them. No doubt many of the emeralds that were known to ancient peoples came from these Egyptian mines.

Emeralds were of much importance in Mexico and Peru, before Columbus found the New World. When the Spaniards conquered Peru, they found great stores of the so-called "Spanish" or "Peruvian" gems. The natives worshiped an emerald (the size of an ostrich egg) which was sacred to the goddess Umina. This was displayed on high feast days when people brought emeralds as offerings to the deity. The priests hid the large emerald so well that the Spaniards were unable to find it. Then the conquerors tried to force the natives to reveal the location of the mines, but neither persecution nor torture could induce them to tell the secret. The natives destroyed all traces of the mines, which were about 75 miles from the city of Bogota. However, in 1558 an inhabitant stumbled upon an emerald; the mines were found and reopened, and have been worked ever since.

However, the Spaniards were able to take back to Spain a large collection of emeralds. Cortez had five special stones, "worked to divers fantastic shapes," which he gave to the niece of the Duke de Bajar. It is reported that Queen Isabella resented this gift, as she wanted the gems for herself. Unluckily, these five choice emeralds were lost at sea when Cortez was shipwrecked on a voyage to help King Charles V at the siege of Algiers.

Numerous magical powers have been attributed to this gem. It was believed, for example, to have mystical healing abilities. One writer during the ninth century declared: "It has power, when mixed with water, to heal leprosy, and other diseases."

An emerald seemed to be a jack of all trades; for it could keep a person honest, sharpen his wits, improve his memory, give him special facility as an orator, and foreshadow coming events. In addition, this stone was a symbol of love, prosperity, kindness, and goodness. Emeralds were known as victory stones, and warriors wore them during battles. Some Indians believed that if they offered an emerald to a god, they would gain "knowledge of the soul of the Eternal."

Once Pliny wrote about a marble lion with eyes of emeralds that adorned a tomb on the Island of Cyprus. Since these jewels shone so brightly, they frightened away the fish from the shore. Therefore, the fishermen removed the emeralds, and replaced them with less brilliant eyes.

The color green has long been considered a restful hue; so it is not surprising that emeralds were thought to be good for one's eyes. Pliny asserted:

If the sight hath been wearied, and dimmed by intensive poring upon something else, the beholding of this stone doth refresh and restore it again.

Nero reputedly used a crystal of emerald to enable him to see the gladiatorial combats in the great arena more clearly. And there is an ancient tale to the effect that emeralds had a fatal effect upon a snake's eyesight—that if the serpent looked upon the stone, it would become blind. In "Lalla Rookh" Thomas Moore wrote:

> Blinded like serpents, when they gaze
> Upon the emerald's virgin blaze.

In historical annals several large fine emeralds have been mentioned. At a French monastery there was one shaped like a cup or dish; some sources believed it was the Holy Grail, used at the Last Supper.

Among the many distinctive emeralds in the Russian crown jewels was an outstanding specimen of more than 135 carats. It was "a deep green in color, with a slight bluish tinge and almost flawless . . . beautifully mounted." The Russians especially liked emeralds. "Their rich green appealed to the almost barbaric love of splendor that underlies Russian taste."

The emerald that is considered the most famous is the "Devonshire." Don Pedro, the last Emperor of Brazil, went to Europe after his abdication. In 1831 he gave the sixth Duke of Devonshire "a splendid natural crystal of emeralds from Muso, in Colombia."

This stone weighed more than 1,383 carats—about ten ounces. Its hue was "the rich grass-green of the true emerald," but unfortunately it had many flaws and a crack across one corner. The Duke of Devonshire exhibited it at the Great Exposition at Hyde Park in 1851; and it was again seen at the White City Show in London in 1936. Later the Duke lent it to the British Museum for display in the mineral gallery in South Kensington.

The emeralds that once belonged to Catherine the Great of Russia are now in the valuable jewel collection (said to be worth several millions) of Barbara Hutton, the Woolworth heiress.

It is said that one of the great emeralds of all time was a square-cut gem weighing between fifty and a hundred carats in Catherine the Great's collection. Another notable item, which featured these beautiful green jewels, was a crown worn by an Indian potentate; emeralds overhung the diadem like bunches of grapes.

Mrs. Norman Winston of New York is the owner of an emerald necklace, once worn by a Queen of Portugal. It is reported that both the Vanderbilt and Rockefeller families had large collections of these distinctive jewels; however, today, they are broken up and owned by various heirs.

According to Eugenia Sheppard, author and Woman's Fashion Editor for the N.Y. *Herald Tribune*, today "emeralds outrank diamonds as glamour stones." At the 1965 opening of the Metropolitan Opera season she noted that: "Mrs. J. H. Heinz, Jr. wore a ring set with a large emerald, also a bib of smaller square-cut gems bought by her husband in India. Mrs. Claude Arpels, dressed in a pale green Paris gown, wore an emerald ensemble—necklace, earrings, and a three-inch wide bracelet." So these outstanding stones, prized since early centuries, still are cherished by those lucky enough to possess them.

May Flower—Lily of the Valley

The lovely lily of the valley has been known for many centuries and is a fragrant plant long cultivated for its delicate odor. According to one source, it expresses "the virtues of purity and humility."

In pagan times, the lily of the valley was the flower of Ostara, the Norse goddess of the dawn. Early Christians dedicated the flower to the Virgin Mary; and it is supposed to have been one of the plants mentioned by Christ, in His Sermon on the Mount.

In some localities the lily of the valley denoted sadness and was termed "Our Lady's Tears." The French named it "The Virgin's Flower." The Irish delighted in the flowers, calling them "fairy ladders," and declared that "the wee folk love to scamper up and down the stems, ringing the bells." Another name given the blossom was "Lily Constancy." In Germany they were called "Little May Bells"; in Sussex, "Bells of Heaven"; and elsewhere, "May Lilies" or "Ladders to Heaven."

Near London, on Hampstead Heath, they used to grow in great abundance; and many Londoners would make excursions out to the Heath to gather them to decorate their churches on Whitsunday, 50 days after Easter.

Generally speaking, lilies of the valley are a northern, rather than a southern flower. The plants—native to England—but not often found there in a wild state, do grow wild in Europe, from Italy to Lapland, and in great profusion in the forests of Germany. The plant is a hardy native of three continents—Western Asia, Europe and the United States, where the wild variety flourishes in the higher Alleghenies, from Virginia to Tennessee.

The perennial lily of the valley grows partly or wholly in shady places, "as if avoiding ruder contacts of the world." The plants—6 to 8 inches in height—thrive in deeply plowed, fertilized soil and are hardy, but the beds must be removed from time to time. The long dark leaves form a good background for the dainty flowers with their delicate fragrance. The erect stem supports the small, nodding, cream-like six-toothed blossoms. When these fade, red berries take their places, and birds enjoy feeding on them.

Most of the cultivated lilies of the valley are grown from roots or "pips" shipped from Europe. In France and Germany florists often force them for the American markets.

In early times some people thought these flowers could cheer one's heart, also help a weak memory. The blooms were used in making love potions. They are still favorites for wedding decorations and for bridal bouquets.

They have been highly prized for hundreds of years for making perfume. "Lily of the Valley Water" was considered so precious that it was kept only in gold or silver containers, and was used to stop the pains of gout or colic, and for sprains. A fine perfume called "Eau d'or" is still made in France from these blossoms.

An old story from Sussex tells that a brave young Christian fought for three days in St. Leonard's forest, with the Dragon, Sin. Finally he was able to repulse the monster. The blood from his wounds fell upon the ground; from the blood spots sprang the fragile, bell-like lilies, in honor of the victory he had won for Christ.

In some places these flowers were associated with the deaths of young lovers; in Germany, with the joy a young man had when visiting his sweetheart and giving her a bouquet of these dainty flowers. However, both young and old will doubtless agree with the early poet who wrote these lines:

> No flower around the garden fairer grows
> Than the sweet lily of the lowly vale,
> The Queen of flowers.

Alternate May Flower—Hawthorn

> The hawthorn bush with seats beneath the shade,
> For talking age and whispering lovers made.
> —OLIVER GOLDSMITH

> And every shepherd tells his tale
> Under the hawthorn in the dale.
> —JOHN MILTON

The hawthorn usually blossoms in May and June. Its masses of lovely flowers—"the snow of the hawthorn"—in white, pink, or crimson, make the English countryside "a thing of beauty and a joy forever."

It is fitting that the hawthorn is one of the flowers dedicated to the month of May. It has always been widespread in the British Isles; and for centuries the English have delighted in going out early on May Day and bringing in great flowering branches to decorate their homes. As a result, the flower was often called the "may."

The popular early poet, Robert Herrick, wrote of this custom:

> There's not a budding boy or girl this May day
> But is got up to bring in May.
> A deal of youth ere this is come
> Back, and with whitethorn laden home . . .

"Hawthorn" is derived from a Greek word meaning "strength." It is so called because its wood is hard and closely grained, therefore taking a fine polish. Various tools and implements, including hammer handles, are made from it. The hawthorn fruit, called "thorn apples," or "haws," looks like miniature apples. Fruits from some kinds of hawthorn are made into preserves and jellies.

The hawthorn is really a shrub or scrubby tree and rarely grows over 25 feet in height. The English have for many years used hawthorn in their gardens for ornamental plants or as hedgerows.

Such trees are found in the temperate regions of the northern hemisphere, in Europe, Africa, and Asia. They have been cultivated widely, and numerous varieties and hybrids have been produced.

Although we may hear more about the English hawthorn, our country, too, has many species. These thrive well in sunny spots; they grow rapidly and are favored for borders in gardens. The state of Missouri has chosen the hawthorn as its flower.

As with other plants, certain stories have become attached to the hawthorn. In Austria, for instance, people believed that this was the plant from which Christ's crown of thorns was made. One legend relates that when Emperor Charlemagne knelt before this crown, which had been preserved, the dry wood at once burst into bloom and the air was fragrant with the lovely scent of hawthorn blossoms.

During that famous Battle of Bosworth Field, the crown of Richard III was hidden in a hawthorn bush. Later, when it had been recovered and placed on Richard's head, he chose as his emblem a crown in a branch of hawthorn.

One of the most famous hawthorns in history is the "Glastonbury Thorn," said to have originated near Glastonbury Abbey. During mild English winters, this hawthorn sometimes bloomed at Christmas time, and the story may have come from this fact.

It was claimed that when Joseph of Arimethea reached England in A.D. 31 with the Holy Grail, he sat down to rest and stuck his staff into the ground. Then a miracle happened: the staff took root and put forth flowers. This phenomenon continued to occur each Christmas after that, and visitors came from long distances to see it and bought slips of the plant at high prices from the monks.

The Puritans presumably resented this superstition and determined to get rid of the plant. One zealot chopped the bush down, but in doing so he cut his leg. A chip also flew up and destroyed the sight of one eye. Tradition declared that even though the trunk and roots were separated, the Glastonbury Thorn continued to grow and blossom. Today, on the grounds of the ruined Abbey, visitors can see this noted plant.

June

After her came jolly June arrayed
All in green leaves, as he a player were . . .
—EDMUND SPENSER

JUNE, our sixth month, was originally the fourth one in the ancient Roman calendar, and had only twenty-six days. Then Romulus gave June four more days; Numa Pompilius took one from it; and finally Julius Caesar restored this month to a period of thirty days.

It is a much debated question as to how June received its name. Some believe the word came from the fact that the month was dedicated to the Juniores or lower branch of the Roman law-making body. Others say it may have been connected with Junius from the Consulate of Junius Brutus.

Leigh Hunt entertained the notion that it was named to honor Juno, wife of Jupiter, king of the gods. Juno was the special deity of women, the goddess of marriage and childbirth. In her honor, the Romans observed a festival on the first of June. (In his writings, Ovid once had Juno say that the month had been named for her.)

The Anglo-Saxons had several names for June; one was "Weyd-monath" because cattle then found good pasturage in the meadows;

another term was "Woed-monath," meaning "weed month"; some of them also named it the "dry month."

According to Leigh Hunt, June is the season of "complete summer":

. . . the hopes of spring are realized; yet the enjoyment is but commenced; we have all summer before us. . . . There is a greater accession of flowers in this month than in any other. . . . The usual business of the month is made up of two employments as beautiful as they are useful—sheepshearing and hay-making.

June has always been considered one of our most desirable periods. Trees and flowers are seen in their new splendor, and in many places the weather is delightful. Coleridge speaks of the "leafy month," of June, while Helen Hunt Jackson exclaims:

> O suns and skies and clouds of June
> And flowers of June together.

Charles H. Towne commented in these lines:

> How softly runs the afternoon
> Beneath the billowy clouds of June,

while John Gould Fletcher described a June evening:

> The evening, blue, voluptuous of June
> Settled slowly on the beach . . .

Someone once declared that "June is the month of greatest summer beauty"; and James Russell Lowell summed it all up by asking and answering a well remembered question:

> And what is so rare as a day in June?
> Then, if ever, come perfect days . . .
> Whether we look or whether we listen,
> We hear life murmur, or see it glisten . . .

Our sixth month has long been a busy one for the farmers, and this is how Clare, in his *Shepherd's Calendar*, described rural scenes at this season:

> The mowers now bend o'er the bearded grass,
> The ploughman sweats along the fallow vale;
> The shepherd's leisure hours are over now
> No more he loiters 'neath the hedge-row bough.

And, while June was a time of great activity for many adults, it was the time when, freed from school, the younger generation enjoyed the freedom of sunny days out-of-doors. In Hone's words:

> Schoolboys, in the brook, disporting
> Spend the sultry hour of play;
> While the nymphs and swains are courting
> Seated in the new-mown hay.

The New England Quaker poet, John Greenleaf Whittier, in his later life looked back on his youth and wrote:

> Oh for boyhood's time of June,
> Crowding years in one brief moon . . .
> I was rich in flowers and trees,
> Humming birds and honey bees . . .
> Laughed the brook for my delight
> Through the day and through the night . . .

Since June is the beginning of the vacation season, when the urge to travel to faraway places takes possession of many persons, Thomas Curtis Clark sings of the joys of this time of the year:

> What a wealth of beauty do I glean . . .
> When June time takes me wandering!

For centuries June has been associated with weddings. It is said that this came about because, since the preceding month was observed for "the unhappy dead," May was considered unlucky for marriages, so weddings usually were postponed until June, and the custom continues.

June is the only month of the twelve in which no President was born; however numerous other important individuals have celebrated their birthdays during this sixth month: Brigham Young, Jefferson Davis, George III, Velasquez, Nathan Hale, Robert Louis Stevenson, John Howard Payne, Prince Philip, Harriet Beecher Stowe, Madame Schumann-Heink, John Wesley, the Duke of Windsor, Helen Keller, John Cabot, and Pearl Buck.

Additional ones are Edvard Grieg, Frank Lloyd Wright, Helen Traubel, Thomas Mann, Anthony Eden, Fred Waring, Pat Boone, Judy Garland, the Empress Josephine (first wife of Napoleon Bonaparte), and Amerigo Vespucci.

Here are some events that took place on different dates in the month of June: in 1683 William Penn made an important treaty with the Indians; in 1692 the people of Salem, Massachusetts hanged their first witch; in 1775 George Washington was made Commander-in-Chief of the Colonial Army; in 1777 the Stars and Stripes became our national ensign; in 1786 ice cream was first advertised; in 1798 the United States passed the first Immigration Act; in 1812 we declared war on Great Britain; and in 1837 Victoria became Queen.

In 1873 the typewriter was invented; in 1876 General Custer made his famous last stand; in 1885 the Statue of Liberty arrived in the United States as a gift from France; in 1896 Henry Ford finished his first motor car; in 1902 the *Twentieth Century Limited*, broke the world's speed limit for long distance runs by covering 148 miles in 145 minutes; and that same year the U.S. purchased the French rights and franchises to the Panama Canal; in 1903 the first cross-country automobile trip began; in 1917 the first Americans reached France to take part in World War I; and in 1919 the first trans-atlantic flight took place.

Also in 1919, the Treaty of Versailles was signed; in 1927 Charles Lindbergh's picture appeared on a U.S. postage stamp—he was the first living American so honored; in 1937 the marriage of the Duke and Duchess of Windsor took place; in 1940 the Germans occupied Paris; in 1944 on D-Day the invasion of France began; in 1945 fifty nations signed the United Nations Charter; and in 1947 came the announcement of the Marshall Plan to help Europe recover from the war.

June contains several holidays that are widely noted in the United States. Many churches celebrate Children's Day on the second Sunday; in Hawaii, on June 11 Kamehameha Day is observed to honor the first king who ruled over the islands. Father's Day, on the third Sunday, brings many family gatherings; while Flag Day on June 14 pays tribute to our national emblem. In some localities St. John's Day is noted when midsummer—June 24—comes around. Two important religious holidays are the Jewish Feast of Weeks (Shavuoth), and Pentecost (Whitsunday), which commemorates the descent of the Holy Spirit on the Apostles in Jerusalem.

June Birthstone—Pearl

> There is many a rich stone laid up in the bowels of the earth, many a fair pearl paid up in the bosom of the sea, that never was seen, nor never shall be.
>
> —JOSEPH HALL

The pearl—emblem of purity—has been held in esteem by various races from very early times. Since primitive man used shellfish for food, naturally it came about that the pearls they found in them were adapted for their own personal adornment. As time passed, pearls were cherished as precious stones and ranked with diamonds, rubies, and sapphires.

These gems were often mentioned in the Bible. The description of the New Jerusalem, in Revelation 21:21, asserts that "the twelve gates were twelve pearls; every several gate was of one pearl." Verse 18:16 describes Babylon as "decked with gold, and precious stones, and pearls"; while in I Timothy 2:9, women are advised not to adorn themselves with "gold, or pearls, or costly array." In Matthew 13:45, 46 Jesus likens the Kingdom of Heaven to "a merchant man seeking goodly pearls; who, when he had found one pearl of great price, went and sold all that he had, and bought it."

Pearls because of their rarity are regarded as gems, but in reality, they are not stones, but the product of shellfish. Pliny mentioned the old belief that pearls were formed by drops of rain falling into oyster shells (while open) and then hardened by animal secretions.

The pearl oyster, a member of the mussel family, fastens itself to rocks or other undersea objects. If a foreign agent—perhaps a grain of sand—gets into the shell, it irritates the soft body. The animal then tries to expel it; if it is not successful, it gradually covers this object with layers of shell material; and so the intruder becomes a beautiful pearl.

These gems are not cut or polished as are other precious stones. The only preparation before use for some pieces of jewelry are the holes that are bored through them. Their hardness varies. The most expensive ones are round; others are pear-shaped or irregular; good color and regularity make them desirable. Pearls are often combined with other gems in jewelry. They must be handled carefully as their lustre can be easily destroyed; also, heat can affect their coloring. As time passes, they become worn looking, and no guaranteed means of preserving them is known.

Pearls differ greatly in coloring—white, black (Indian gems are sometimes tinged with yellow), salmon-pink, red, brown, or a blackish cream. Those with a rosy sheen, mostly from the Persian Gulf, are the highest prized and most expensive. These, termed Oriental pearls, have "a shimmering lustre from below the surface caused by the effect of reflected and refracted light from the various layers." Black and greenish tinged pearls are rare and valuable; Venezuela has produced some of the former. Since pearls do vary in color, a well-matched strand has sold for as much as a million dollars.

From early times, the main source for pearls was and still is—for the lovely Oriental pearls especially—the Persian Gulf off the coast of Arabia. During certain months the natives gather the gems, which are sent to Bombay and to the markets of Europe. Other localities for this industry include the Gulf of Manaar, near Ceylon, from which come small silvery pearls of high quality; the northern and western shores of Australia, and at some Pacific islands off the coast of Venezuela, New Guinea, Borneo, and the noted Pearl Islands, not far from the Pacific opening of the Panama Canal. Often black pearls have been discovered on the Mexican coast, along Lower California.

In addition to those found along the seashore, some of these jewels have come from fresh waters. Excellent specimens were found in the rivers of Scotland. Several of the best ones from this source have been mounted in the Scottish Crown Jewels, kept in Edinburgh Castle. An especially fine pearl from the Conway River in North Wales—now in the Royal Crown—was presented to the wife of Charles II.

During the Middle Ages, pearls from fresh water were used as medicine. Centuries ago, when there was little real knowledge of medicine, these gems were believed to restore health. A thirteenth-century doctor of Castile wrote:

The pearl is most excellent in the medical art, for it is of great help in palpitation of the heart, and those who are sad or timid are helped in every sickness which is caused by melancholia, because it purifies the blood, clears it and removes all impurities.

Even as late as the seventeenth century some people retained the belief that pearls could restore a person's strength. Lorenzo de Medici, for example, was given some of these jewels in his last illness. The famous philosopher, Francis Bacon, was of the opinion that pearls could lengthen life.

Pearls have long played an important role in the lives of royal personages. Roman rulers paid high prices for such stones; Caligula is said to have worn slippers made of pearls; and it is reported that in Pompey's triumphal procession thirty-three rulers' crowns made of pearls were carried. Nero in his theatre had actors use pearl sceptres.

Queen Marie Antoinette of France had an outstanding collection of pearls; later some of them became the property of the American wife of the eighth Duke of Marlborough. (The ill-fated French Queen's noted pearls are now the property of Barbara Hutton, who also owns the yellow pearls once worn by the Empress of Japan.)

Elizabeth II seems to have a preference for pear-shaped pearl earrings.

Mrs. Jack Gardner had seven strings of pearls, which in her lifetime became almost as well known as her fabulous art gallery in Boston. Sometimes she wore all of them in one long rope that fell to her knees.

When the great artist Sargent painted her portrait, which can be seen today at Fenway Court, he had her wear a severely plain black gown. Then the painter persuaded her to take her pearls, with a large ruby pendant, from her neck, and drape them around her waist—an unusual and unforgettable touch.

The story of Cleopatra and the pearl is well known. At an expensive banquet that she was giving for Antony, she took off a pearl eardrop, dissolved it in wine and drank to the health of the Roman triumvir.

A similar story is told in connection with Elizabeth I of England: When visiting Sir Thomas Gresham at the Royal Exchange, he pledged her health in a cup of wine in which a pearl, valued at 15,000 pounds had been placed. (However, since authorities maintain that vinegar does not dissolve pearls, and that a drink with a stronger acid in it would not be suitable to drink, perhaps we must discount these stories.)

Shakespeare advanced another idea—that pearls are connected with tears, when he wrote in *Richard III:*

> The liquid drops of tears that you have shed
> Shall come again, transferred to Orient pearl.

Some of the largest pearls ever found include one in the Hope Collection; it was two inches long, weighed over 454 carats, and sold for 12,000 pounds. A perfectly round, 28-carat pearl, the Pellegrina, was on view in the Moscow Museum. Several exceptional specimens are in the famous collection in the Green Vault in Dresden, while a three ounce gem is shown at the South Kensington Museum. An Australian pearl found in October, 1911, weighed 178 grains and sold for 3,000 pounds.

At a recent Festival of Oriental Art an exquisite Oriental pearl was displayed. This was said to be the largest one in the world; it has been authenticated by the American Gem Society as the most perfect one known for its size, which is one and one-half inches by one inch, by one-half inch.

This unusual pearl, valued at $50,000 was brought to Hong Kong when a wealthy family fled there from Red China. A jewelry industry official, Michael Mendelson, bought it for his wife. It is mounted in platinum, accented by 21 diamonds, and is worn as a pendant.

Today the pearl oysters along the Japanese coast have been induced to create these jewels by the "deliberate introduction of a foreign substance." This idea of "culturing" pearls is an old one, but it wasn't until about sixty years ago that this now important Japanese industry became successful, because of the experiments made by Kokichi Mikimoto. The workers in this industry insert perfectly round balls made of clam shells from our own Mississippi River, since those in Japan are not hard enough. The "seeded" oysters are suspended in wire baskets in warm coastal waters. It takes the oysters from three to five years to produce these cultured pearls.

There is quite a difference in the prices of natural and cultured pearls. The former are said to retain their natural sheen and form longer than the cultured ones. However, one expert said of the cultured gems: "that they are chemically the same as the natural pearl cannot be denied."

Alternate June Birthstone—Moonstone

The moonstone, an alternate gem for June, belongs to the important mineral family, the feldspar. Others of this group are sometimes used as semi-precious stones, but the moonstone, with its lovely bloom, alone is commonly used as a jewel.

It is the most popular member of the family. Its exquisite sheen has been compared to the radiance of moonlight—hence its name. The sheen is due to its unusual structure, for it is a combination of thin layers of materials. This stone is transparent, often colorless, but also is found with "a milky sheen and bluish opalescence." These are attributed to the lights reflected from the stone's various layers.

The white, rather pale ones, are not of much value, but those with the coveted "blue bloom" are valuable and much desired. There is a regular market only for the scarce type, the ones with the bluish cast. Although these gems are rather soft, they are used in limited numbers for rings. The stones are cut en cabochon and are never faceted.

The chief sources of supply for moonstones have for many years been Southern and Central Ceylon, where the gems are found in large quantities in gem-bearing gravels. Others of fairly good quality have come from the St. Gotthard district of Switzerland. In recent years, moonstones have also been discovered in Burma, Madagascar, and Tanganyika.

One writer, Herbert S. Whitlock, believes that "as material for necklace beads, the unique beauty of this gem stone does not seem to be fully appreciated."

Second Alternate June Birthstone—Alexandrite

The alexandrite, another alternate stone for June, is a very unusual and interesting one. Grass-green, in some cases, it is a variety of chrysoberyl, and is distinguished by its "chameleon-like quality." This peculiar trait causes these stones of dark green or grayish green by daylight to change to a raspberry or columbine red when viewed under artificial light. This is due to the fact that the alexandrite absorbs more of the red part of the spectrum that is stronger in the artificial light.

These stones were first found in 1833 in emerald mines near Ekaterinburg, in the Ural Mountains of Russia on the day when the man who later ruled as Alexander II was celebrating his coming of age. Therefore, the stone was named in his honor. The red and green shades in this gem were the colors of the old Imperial Russian Army, and for nearly one hundred years, it was the acknowledged national gem of Russia.

Alexandrites are among the most valuable of all semi-precious stones. Naturally they have been most highly prized by the Russians. Those from the Urals are of a bluish or greenish shade, but not so many come from that source now. Those from Ceylon—the chief source of supply today—are not considered as attractive as the ones from Russia. The Ceylonese stones are usually a deep olive green in hue, are more transparent, have less contrast in the absorption color, and are larger.

Alexandrites have also been discovered in South Rhodesia, Madagascar, Upper Burma (some yellow ones in Brazil), and in the United States at Haddam, Connecticut; and Greenfield, New York.

These distinctive stones are harder than others except for the diamond and corundum, making them suitable for use in jewelry, including finger rings. When alexandrites are mounted with diamonds, there is a fine contrast. Stones of five carats or more are quite rare. Because of this scarcity, the gems command high prices, and cost from eight to twenty-five pounds per carat (about twenty-two dollars to seventy dollars).

One source states that there are synthetic alexandrites on the market that "are really either synthetic sapphires or synthetic spinels, the color being due to an oxide of vanadium and not to a chromium oxide as in the natural stone." By artificial light they change to a purple-red, or amethyst hue, from greenish-red in daylight.

The alexandrite is one of the most intriguing of all gemstones. G. F. Herbert Smith in his book, *Gemstones,* tells us:

The dull fires that seem to glow within them in ordinary daylight, and the curious change in color, which affects them when seen by artificial illumination, add a touch of mystery to these dark stones.

June Flower—Rose

> The rose that lives its little hour
> Is prized beyond the sculptured flower.
> —WILLIAM CULLEN BRYANT

The rose, dedicated to June, has been termed "man's favorite flower," and the "queen of flowers." This well-beloved blossom has been known and cherished since ancient times.

Roses grow all through the north temperate zone, as far south as Abyssinia, Eastern India, and Mexico, in fact, everywhere, except in the Arctic regions, and along the equator.

The rose family is a large one, and includes such plants as the apple and cherry trees. For many centuries, roses have been crossed and recrossed until countless species have been developed in a variety of habits, sizes, and colorings. Our present-day roses are descendants of wild ones, whose numerous leaves have been lessened, and the blooms enlarged. The early species are classed into two major divisions: bush and clinging types. The cultivation of roses is a big industry nowadays; with some growers dealing exclusively in these flowers.

The plant is said to be as old as civilization itself, for roses were known in China and in Persia centuries ago. The famous King Midas developed types with lovely fragrance and as many as sixty petals. The Romans called this blossom the "Flower of Venus," and dedicated it to the goddess of the dawn.

The Romans had such extensive rose gardens that Horace was prompted to mention the lack of space for growing vegetables. Rose leaves were sprinkled on the ashes of the dead; and Romans often provided in their wills that roses should be planted at their tombs. Shrines and arches were entwined with these flowers. It is said that Italy has produced some very tall rose bushes, one of which grew to the height of sixty feet.

The sybarites (lovers of luxury and pleasure) in Rome slept on beds stuffed with rose petals. They wore as necklaces wreaths of these flowers and had fountains from which rose water flowed.

Nero was a noted lover of roses. It is said that he spent as much as $150,000 for these flowers for a single feast. His guests bathed in marble-lined pools, in rose-scented water.

Toulouse in France was associated with roses, and one story tells that a single plant there produced 60,000 blooms. The city was notable for its yearly poetry contest. On one such occasion, Mary, Queen of Scots, sent a silver rose for the winner. At other French localities there were festivals dedicated to this plant; one important feature was the crowning of a Rose Queen. Golden or silver roses were often given as gifts by royalty, or by the Pope, for special services.

The rose for centuries has been a symbol of silence; and it is reported that Cupid gave Harpocrates, the god of silence, a rose as a bribe not to tell of the secret love affairs of Venus, goddess of love. Today, we still use the Latin expression, *sub rosa*, for something told in confidence. This dates back to 479 B.C. when the Greeks defeated Xerxes of Persia. It is asserted that the decisive battle was planned in a rose garden near Minerva's Temple. Following this affair, often a rose was hung over a table (or roses were carved in the ceiling) in the room where secret business was to be transacted.

One of the most famous rosebushes in all history is still growing and producing flowers in Hildesheim, Germany. The story is that more than ten centuries ago—in 814—Ludwig the Pious, with his knights and dogs, assembled for a day of hunting. Everyone was eager to be off to the chase, and waited impatiently while a priest asked God's blessing on the knives, spears, and dogs. As soon as the "Amen" was said, the party galloped away without partaking of the holy bread and wine which the priest had placed on the ground. The following day a rosebush was discovered covering the sacrament. It grew miraculously; and Ludwig the Pious ordered a church to be built by it.

On March 22, 1945, when Hildesheim was bombed, the cathedral fell in flames; the rose branches were destroyed, but the roots were unharmed, and again, in June, 1946, the bush produced leaves and flowers. There is a local legend to the effect that as long as this rosebush exists so will the city of Hildesheim. It was largely destroyed during World War II, but it has been rebuilt and is now flourishing. The town has as its emblem the thousand-year old rosebush.

When we think of roses and their part in history, naturally the famous "Wars of the Roses" come to mind. These conflicts extended through about thirty years of English history, during the reigns of Henry VI, Edward IV, and Richard III. They were fought between the House of York whose symbol was the white rose; and that of Lancaster, represented by a red rose.

The white rose had been adopted by Eleanor of Provence, who married Henry III of England in 1236; and her son, Edward I, incorporated it into the Great Seal of the State. The red rose was the symbol of Edmund, first Earl of Lancaster. About the end of the thirteenth century he brought back from France a red rose that had originated in Damascus and took it as his emblem. The rose was also adopted by his two nephews, the sons of King Edward I.

The Wars of the Roses began in 1455, when the rival Houses of York and Lancaster plucked red and white roses from the Temple Gardens in London. This conflict cost the lives of 100,000 men. Henry Tudor of Lancaster defeated and killed Richard III, the last Yorkist monarch, at the Battle of Bosworth Field, on August 22, 1485, thus ending the last of the Wars of the Roses.

Henry VII married Elizabeth, Duchess of York, daughter of Edward IV, and started a new line of British rulers. The Tudor rose, now the English floral emblem, came as a combination of the two roses.

It is said that, at the time of this union, in a monastery garden in Wiltshire, a rose bloomed with both red and white petals. Up to this time, it had had red blooms on some branches and white on others. The custom of laying a sword on a bed of roses on Christmas Day in memory of the Wars of the Roses was practiced in London for some time.

From primitive times roses were used in medicines, foods, and perfumes. Pliny stated that there were twelve remedies made from rose leaves and petals, including a wine that was good for nervous-ness. Sleeping on a pillow filled with dried rose leaves was also believed to help victims of this disease, while rose ointment could alleviate pain. Pliny told of a young soldier who had been bitten by a mad dog. This was revealed to his mother in a dream; then she sent her son a dog rose, and he was cured.

Some sources say that more roses have been used in making perfume than any other flowers. This is an important European industry; and at the noted perfume center at Grasse, France, 950 tons of roses have been used in comparison with 147 tons of violets. Simple rose water was long popular in England as a scent, and was often used as an air conditioner. This liquid was also an ingredient in a concoction labeled "Water that makes a face look young." Rose water was used in a dentrifice, perhaps for the first time, in Great Britain.

Oil of roses—attar of roses—is essential in the manufacture of perfume. An Arabian doctor named Avicenna in 1187 discovered a method of making it by distillation.

Rose seeds or "hips" look like small apples. In medieval days ladies used them in desserts, in salads, on meats, and flavored quince preserves with them. Rose leaves combined with sugar and spice made a coveted conserve. The hips were also used in making vinegar, syrup, and cordials.

At royal banquets in bygone centuries, there was a special dessert, called "soltylty" (subtlety), which was a "monumental piece of culinary sculpture constructed of paste, sugar, and gelatine." Such a delicacy often was made with a paste of roses and decorated with candied rose petals. One of these was prepared especially for the feast after the coronation of Henry V and his queen.

For ages roses have inspired writers, both of prose and poetry; and artists. All over the globe, stories, legends, songs, poems, and pictures have been connected with these flowers.

Marcus Aurelius wrote ". . . familiar as the rose in spring"; James Montgomery, "The rose has but a summer reign"; Richard

Ryan, "Her cheek is like the rose is, but fresher, I ween"; Keats, "Sudden a thought came like a full blown rose." Christina Rossetti declared, "Love is like a lovely rose, the world's delight." And the world will always remember those famous lines written by Robert Burns:

> O, my love is like a red, red rose
> That's newly sprung in June.

This flower was mentioned in the Song of Solomon (2:1) although some authorities say it was probably not the same plant; in Isaiah we read that the wilderness shall "blossom as the rose."

This flower, considered a symbol of purity, was often associated with the Virgin Mary, and in various paintings she was shown with a rose in her hand. During the Middle Ages, there was a "Rose Sunday" because of the belief, that after Mary ascended to Heaven, roses and lilies filled her tomb. Roses also adorned the brows of martyred saints in works of art.

In heraldry, roses often were depicted; they were popular too in stained glass windows, in draperies, and in dress materials. Frequently royalty used them in jewelry, where they were surrounded by precious stones. In the period of some early English kings, roses appeared in their crowns.

One of the most interesting stories connected with this flower is that of the famous Pennsylvania glassmaker, Baron William Stengel. In 1772 he stated in his will that the German Lutheran Church (the Zion Lutheran at Mannheim), which he had given the congregation, should pay his descendants on demand a single red rose as rent for the yearly use of the structure.

It is interesting to note the way trends in roses—just as in clothes—have changed. During the Victorian period pink roses were the favorites of most persons. Later in the 1890's, the "Gibson Girl," immortalized by the artist, Charles Dana Gibson, was associated with the deep, richly colored American Beauty rose.

American colonists imported roses from Britain for their formal gardens and also developed different types of their own. It is said that George Washington produced a truly American rose, the hybrid, "Martha Washington."

In the United States countless new varieties have been produced and have won high awards. Each one means years of work, during which numerous plants have been discarded in efforts to evolve new shades or structures. One authority says that California growers have produced more new ones and have won more awards than the Eastern States and Europe together.

One source estimates that more than $5,000,000 is spent annually in private U.S. research involving ornamental horticulture, and that when a new variety of plant appears, it may have cost its originator between $50,000 and $75,000 to produce.

Each June fanciers eagerly await the announcement from the All-American Rose Selections, Inc., of the rose, or roses, that the judges have chosen as worthy of the title of "All-American Rose Selection."

In 1962 it was announced that four great new roses had been honored: the "John S. Armstrong," a dark and velvety red which climaxed twenty years of research by the Armstrong Nurseries of Ontario, California, "to develop a hybrid that embraces all the qualities and characteristics one could reasonably desire in a rose." This winner was named to honor the eighty-five-year old founder and chairman of the California rose-breeding farm. One writer declared that "the vivid red quality of the J. S. Armstrong's flower adds a new color to the universal rose spectrum."

The three other winners were the "Christian Dior," a red hybrid tea rose by Conrad Pyle; the "King's Ransom," a yellow tea rose by Jackson and Perkins Company; and "Golden Slippers," a fluorescent orange and gold tone by Peterson and Dering.

Of the next year's winner, Harry Golden made this statement:

Royal Highness, a clear light pink, has captured the coveted award and will carry the distinguished honor of 1963 All-America Rose, along with another hybrid tea, Tropicana. . . . In every way Royal Highness is an exhibitor's delight, as well as a stunning showpiece in the garden.

This rose was developed by a noted hybridist, Herbert Swim, and has not only exquisite beauty but a delightful fragrance.

The other winner, "Tropicana," a hybrid tea variety, was developed by a German, Mathias Tantau, and introduced into the United States by Jackson and Perkins. It is "a vibrant orange-red beauty and far exceeds its forebears in vigor, hardiness, disease resistance, and brilliancy of color."

It is said that this rose will last up to two weeks, and, when cut for indoor use, has an average life of one week. The blooms may be as much as five inches in size; and they have a delightful spicy fragrance. The Tropicana is adaptable to all parts of the United States. By the beginning of February, 1963, this rose had already won fourteen top awards in America and other countries. One authority stated of it:

If all the hybridists in the world were to get together and describe the ideal rose—it would be Tropicana. This is the variety that every rose hybridist dreams about.

One All-American Rose in 1964 was "Granada," a multi-colored hybrid tea rose, produced by a Southern Californian, Robert V. Lindley. He "achieved a new breakthrough in sparkling color combinations and spicy fragrance." The Granada was termed "a colorful, new champion that blazes with colors found in a matador's cape." This rose is also acclaimed for its fragrance.

The other winner, "Saratoga," is quite a contrast; for it is famed for its pure white richness which is difficult for a breeder to achieve. This was only the fifth white rose to win in the twenty-four years the selections have been made. Saratoga blooms abundantly, produces large flowers, is long lasting, and its sweet scent adds much to its appeal.

Continuing progress in rose culture was shown when the winners for 1965 were announced—"Camelot" and "Mister Lincoln." These had both won awards in earlier major competitions.

After many years our great Civil War President was honored by having a distinctive rose named for him. The Mister Lincoln is a hybrid tea rose—deep, velvety, with a delightful fragrance. The flowers, often six inches across, have more than forty large thick petals. The plants bloom freely during the summer months. Mister Lincoln is "a vigorous, well branched one that truly does honor to Abraham Lincoln." It was developed by Swim and Weeks of Ontario, California.

Camelot, "a luminous coral pink grandiflora rose," is a queenly blossom, and "well named for the lovely ladies and gallant knights of the ancient and storied city of King Arthur and his court." The opened blossoms measure five inches in diameter, and exude a rich spicy odor. These roses are tall and vigorous, with deep green foliage. Camelot is a worthy descendant of two noted roses: the "Queen Elizabeth" and "Circus."

Two other outstanding roses—new in 1965—are the "Polynesian Sunset" and the "John F. Kennedy."

Polynesian Sunset was selected as "Rose of the Year" for 1965, by a panel of 15,000 American home gardeners after they had observed it for a year. The blooms are at first a deep coral, which gradually change to a coral-orange, three inches across. One plant produced fifty-nine blooms between June and October.

The John F. Kennedy, a sparkling white rose of classic form, has been named as a living memorial to the late President. One Illinois man wrote of it:

This is the best white hybrid tea I've ever had in my garden as far as flower form, lasting quality, and plant vigor are concerned. It lasts indefinitely as a cut flower, and seems to increase in beauty each day.

Three beautiful new roses have already been named as the 1966 All-America roses "Matterhorn," "Apricot Nectar," and "American Heritage."

The Matterhorn, grown by Armstrong Nurseries, is a white hybrid with sturdy, medium-sized blooms on long stems. The vigorous plant will stand all types of weather. The color varies from ivory to pure white, forming an excellent contrast to its glossy, green foliage.

Apricot Nectar, a floribunda, has a fruity odor, and large clusters of blossoms. The buds are a soft apricot, but the petals lighten as the flowers open.

American Heritage is distinctive and presents a changing pageant of color. At first the buds are a light yellow, but as they open, there is a touch of crimson on the edges of the petals. This new variety was developed by Dr. Walter Lammerts and introduced on the market by Germain's.

In addition to these three outstanding roses, other newly developed ones are "Strawberry Blonde," "Gaytime," "Hallmark," and "Simon Bolivar," named for the noted South American patriot.

According to recent news, the "Rose of 1966" is the "Mexicana," the "best of some 100,000 seedlings that first bloomed eight years ago."

It is reported that 15,000 home rose growers have tested this rose in varying temperatures, climates, soils, etc., and that "Mexicana under all circumstances has behaved like a true thoroughbred."

This winner is an intensely red hybrid tea rose; when opened, it has a spread of five and one-half inches or more; it blooms freely; and has an old-fashioned fragrance.

So with all these new varieties, it seems that rose lovers will never lack for beauty and variety in their gardens.

Someone recently wrote this in regard to roses:

There is no more rewarding plant for garden and landscape than roses. They will grow anywhere in the fifty states where the sun shines. Their blooming season in most areas will be six months or even more, far longer than most other garden flowers.

Some cities in America are renowned for their dedication to this flower, and two distinctive events illustrating this devotion take place at Pasadena, California and at Portland, Oregon annually.

The first Rose Parade was held in Pasadena on January 1, 1886, under the sponsorship of Charles F. Holder, founder of the Valley Hunt Club. That day members of the organization adorned their horse-drawn vehicles with cut roses and other flowers, took part in a parade, and then attended athletic events. Finally the city of Pasadena took over the project, and the Tournament of Roses Association was formed as a permanent sponsor.

In the beginning there was varied entertainment, such as chariot races, etc. but now a football contest between east and west teams is the main attraction after the parade. Naturally there is a beautiful queen, with her charming attendants. Each year the affair has become more elaborate; and since only fresh blooms are permitted, the decorations for a single float often cost several thousands of dollars.

Each year there is a different theme; the floats, some from distant cities, carry out the current motif. In addition, there are many brilliant bands, horsemen on prancing steeds including distinctive palominos with glittering silver trappings—all led by the Grand Marshal, a nationally known celebrity. This outstanding event at Pasadena draws more than a million visitors annually.

Since 1907, Portland, Oregon has also staged a noted Rose Festival each year, but as early as 1889 the Portland Rose Society had its first exhibition of roses. In 1904 they put on a floral parade with carriages, bicycles, and *four* cars. Three years later, the idea of a yearly affair was agreed upon, and the Rose Festival Association was incorporated.

The purpose of this yearly event is "To promote Portland and Oregon as the rose capital of the world, and to promote the rose." In Washington Park, high above the city, is the International Rose Test Garden, with more than 10,000 rose bushes, including more than 500 varieties.

At first, a man, "Rex Oregonus," ruled over the event; but in 1914, he was replaced by a Rose Queen, in the "Rule of Rosaria." Each year thousands of out-of-towners throng to Portland to see this great community spectacle. In the parade are gorgeous allegorical floats, bands, members of varied organizations, and thousands of school children making this beautiful festival honoring the "Queen of Flowers" a most enjoyable affair.

The state flower of New York is the rose; that of Iowa, the wild rose; North Dakota, prairie rose; Georgia, the Cherokee rose; and the District of Columbia, the American Beauty. Strange to say, the United States, like Russia, does not have a national flower. Various Congressmen have tried to remedy this from time to time. In 1959 American Florists held a nation-wide contest to discover which flower our people really preferred. When all the votes were in (1,055,629 voters participated) it was found that the rose had won; that it was a two-to-one favorite over the carnation. Runners-up were the chrysanthemum, lily of the valley, orchid, tulip, and gladiolus in that order.

Senator Hugh Scott of Pennsylvania declared that the rose is "a solid tradition" with Americans; Senator Margaret Chase Smith of Maine wears a rose corsage every day. So it is to be hoped that the United States will soon choose a floral emblem in accordance "with the will of the people."

Alternate June Flower—Honeysuckle

> The Wild Honeysuckle
> Fair flower, that dost so comely grow,
> Hid in this silent, dull retreat,
> Untouched thy honied blossomed blow,
> Unseen thy little branches greet . . .
> Unpitying frosts and Autumn's power
> Shall leave no vestige of this flower.
> —Philip Freneau

Whenever we hear the word honeysuckle we naturally think of a lovely fragrant vine, with flowers of white, yellow, pink to purple, or scarlet hue.

The early name of this plant was "woodbine," and this is still used in some localities. Honeysuckle, native to the Northern Hemisphere, grows in Europe, Asia, and North America; it has 175 species, and about twenty-five are found in Canada and the United States.

Some honeysuckles are tall, scrubby bushes and grow in woods, or along roadways. Others have been introduced into gardens; many have been cultivated as ornamental vines, and trained over fences, porches, trellises, or windows, adding attraction around homes.

The most common species is the Tartarian honeysuckle, which may grow to a height of ten feet. In June it has rose-pink blossoms, and in the fall, bright red berries. The common name of the red variety is the trumpet honeysuckle, a good climber. This is a favorite with humming birds, for the trumpet contains nectar, and the fragrance attracts these tiny birds. One type, a bush with small yellow blooms, is a mecca for bees.

Honeysuckle leaves are oval; and most varieties are evergreen. When the flowers drop off, red berries take their places. Since birds eat them, honeysuckles are widely distributed; insects, too, carry pollen to the plants. In the eastern part of our country the Japanese honeysuckle, native to Eastern Asia, has escaped from culture and grows wild in many places. When this plant has established its roots, there is no holding it back, in fact, in some states it is considered a pest. Honeysuckle wood is hard, and is sometimes used for making canes and the teeth of rakes.

For centuries the honeysuckle has been popular, and not only for its fragrance. Some people during medieval times raised the vines for medicinal purposes in their castle gardens. In addition, they made "distilled water" or (perfume) from the petals; the blooms were used in a conserve, that was said to be beneficial to one's health. Years ago, in rural districts, the leaves were crushed and applied to bee stings to reduce soreness.

In her book, *Lady with Green Fingers*, the author, Bea Howe states:

To discourage evil spirits from entering the house, she (the country housewife) brought back honeysuckle (or fairy trumpets) from the woods and set it to twine round the porch-posts of her home. Honeysuckle was also used to protect cows from harm and to keep the milk and butter sweet.

An interesting Italian legend gives us the origin of the honeysuckle: A young peasant, Paolo, fell in love with two girls, one a blonde, the other a brunette. Both Bianca and Nerina loved Paolo, but they had promised each other not to be jealous, no matter whom he chose.

When he threw bouquets into their gardens, Bianca did not return the attention, but Nerina did, without telling her friend. Since Paolo couldn't make up his mind, he vowed to wed the girl who first gave him a flower. At that season, all plants were dead; at once Bianca prayed for flowers; and when her tears watered the earth, a graceful vine grew from them—the first honeysuckle ever seen.

Bianca prayed to Venus to help her; and as a result, the next morning the vine was covered with blooms. When Paolo passed, he smelled the lovely fragrance, and paid no attention to the kisses that Nerina was sending in his direction. At once, he went toward Bianca and kissed her, all because of the perfume sent forth by the honeysuckle.

In Shakespeare's time honeysuckle (believed to be under the rule of Mercury) was considered "a favorite remedy for wounds in the head." In *Much Ado about Nothing*, the Bard of Avon says:

> Bid her steal into the pleached bower,
> Where honeysuckles, ripened by the sun,
> Forbid the sun to enter.

And in *Midsummer Night's Dream*, he entwined Titania's canopy with "luscious woodbine." Another writer put it this way: "The honeysuckle is a flower that belongs particularly to moonlight and fairyland."

July

Now comes July, and with his fervid noon
Unsinews labor . . . the faint steer,
Lashing his sides, draws sulkily along
The slow encumbered wain in midday heat.
—EDMUND SPENSER

JULY, our seventh month, was in fifth place on the early Roman calendar. At first it was named *Quintilis* (fifth) and had thirty-six days. Romulus reduced it to thirty-one, and Numa Pompilius to thirty. Later Julius Caesar restored one day, giving it thirty-one.

During Caesar's consulate Mark Antony had tried to make him Emperor, but without success. So Antony complimented him by naming the fifth month for him, as Caesar's birthday fell on the fourteenth. Thus the month became July in 44 B.C., the very year he was stabbed by Brutus.

Of the occasion Leigh Hunt wrote:

July is so named after Julius Caesar, who contrived to divide his time between months and dynasties, and among his better deeds of ambition, reformed the calendar.

And one authority tells us that until the beginning of the nineteenth-century "July" was pronounced with the accent on the first syllable, keeping to its origin from "Julius."

Since it was so sultry in Italy at this season, many Romans became ill; therefore a superstition arose that July heat and resulting sicknesses were connected with the rising and setting of Canicula (the Little Dog Star). The period from July 3 to August 11 was known as the "dog days," a term still in use.

The poet Horace told of a famous garnet that was engraved with the face of a dog; its tongue was hanging out; and the head was surrounded by the rays of the sun. This was probably an allusion to "dog days" depicted in jewelry.

Another early writer referred to the July heat in these lines:

> Then came July, hot, boiling like to fire,
> That all his garments he had cast away,
> Upon a lyon, raging yet with ire,
> He boldly rode, and made him to obey.

And as another wrote: "July is a large portion of the year, which is made glorious summer by the sun"; then there is "full summer" accompanied by great heat.

Our Anglo-Saxon forebears had more than one name for July, including "Mead-monath"; for then the meadows were in full bloom and cattle enjoyed good pasturage. Another term was "Hey-monath" as they gathered in the hay at this period. Sometimes, too, they called July "Hen-monath," which *may* have denoted "foliage month."

> Our Saxon fathers did full regularly call
> This month of July, "haymonath" when all
> The verdure of the full-clothed fields we mow,
> And turn and rake and carry off; and so
> We build it up, in large and solid mows
> If it be good, as everybody knows,
> To "make hay while the sun shines," we should choose
> "Right times for all things" and no time abuse.

A modern poet, Ralph W. Seager, has spoken of July in these lines:

> The opulent harvest crowds upon the field . . .
> Stretching its fences with the golden yield.

After this seasonal work has been finished, and the hay has been stowed away for winter use . . .

> The mower now gives labor o'er
> And on his bench beside the door
> Sits down to watch his children play,
> Smoking a leisure hour away.

Although as Sarah Coolidge says, "Hot July brings cooling showers," it is also the season of thunderstorms. In regard to this, William Hone quotes an early poet:

> Maids, with each a guardian lover,
> While the vivid lightning flies,
> Hastening to the nearest cover,
> Clasp their hands before their eyes.

July, too, is the month when various grains ripen; and in many localities farmers are busy harvesting. But "those who can avoid labor enjoy as much rest and shade as possible."

Calvin Coolidge appropriately "first saw the light of day" on Independence Day, July 4, while John Quincy Adams celebrated his birthday on July 11.

Other persons of note who were born during July are Nathaniel Hawthorne, Stephen Foster, P. T. Barnum, Cecil Rhodes, Count von Zeppelin, Julius Caesar, Josiah Wedgwood, Henry D. Thoreau, Rembrandt, Sir Joshua Reynolds, John Paul Jones, William M. Thackeray, Ernest Hemingway, Simon Bolivar, George Bernard Shaw, Corot, Mussolini, Henry Ford, Kirsten Flagstad, Dr. Charles H. Mayo, Isaac Watts, Amelia Earhart, John Jacob Astor, Dag Hammarskjold, Ginger Rogers, Henry Cabot Lodge, Jr., Louis Armstrong, Garibaldi, Nelson Rockefeller, John Calvin, and John Wanamaker.

In July 1604, the King James version of the Bible was authorized; in 1619 our first elected legislature was chosen at Jamestown,

Virginia; in 1775 Congress established the U.S. postal service; in 1777 Lafayette was given a commission in the Continental Army; in 1788 Congress created the Marine Corps; in 1790 the District of Columbia was set up; that same year the first U.S. patent was issued; 1802 saw the opening of the U.S. Military Academy at West Point.

In 1826, on July 4, both John Adams and Thomas Jefferson died; in 1832 "America" was sung for the first time; in 1848 the cornerstone of the Washington Monument was laid; also in that year the first Women's Rights' Convention met at Seneca Falls, New York; in 1858, the first baseball series began; in 1861 the Battle of Bull Run took place; in 1863 came the surrender of Vicksburg; also that same year the Battle of Gettysburg was fought; and in 1865 General William Booth founded the Salvation Army.

The year 1866 witnessed the first successful laying of an Atlantic cable; in 1898 Hawaii was annexed to the United States; in 1903 Henry Ford sold his first automobile; in 1914 the First World War began; in 1920 there was the official opening of the Panama Canal; in 1937 Amelia Earhart disappeared; in 1945 the first nuclear explosion was heard; and in 1938 "Wrong Way" Corrigan flew solo to Ireland.

July, our seventh month, is an important one in American history; during it, in 1776, the Declaration of Independence was issued, proclaiming our break with the mother country, England. July 4 is a legal holiday in all states and territories, and throughout the country varied celebrations take place.

Jean O. Mitchell has well expressed the feeling that is felt by many Americans in regard to Independence Day:

> The Fourth of July was *the day* of the year
> When I was a child on the farm . . .

July 15 has long been observed in England as St. Swithin's Day. According to an old belief, if it rains on this date, there will be forty more rainy days following it. July 30 has been set apart as Joseph Lee Day, to honor the "Father of the Playground Movement."

July Birthstone—The Ruby

Because of its rich glowing color, the ruby is considered by many to be the most beautiful of gems. Its name comes from the Latin, *ruber*, through its later form, *rubinus*, which denotes "red." An early writer spoke of it as follows:

. . . the ruby, called the Lord of gems and highly prized, the dearly loved ruby, so fair with its gay color.

However, this stone was included, and confused, by Romans with other red gems (spinel and garnet), under the name, *carbunculus*, and by the Greeks, with *anthrax*, both of which mean "a burning coal."

It is said that the first reference to the word ruby was in 1310 in the *Oxford Dictionary;* and in 1380 Chaucer wrote, ". . . lyke ruby ben your chekys rounde."

This popular and costly gem is usually found in six-sided crystals. Natural rubies are discovered in two kinds of association; in Burma, they occur in limestone rock, and in Ceylon, in gravel deposits. The ruby contains iron oxide which gives it the red color; it is translucent and transparent, and varies in hardness and hue according to the locality where it is found. Large, perfect rubies are very rare, as most of the stones have flaws. Some cloudy or opaque rubies of attractive coloring may be used effectively for jewelry, when cut en cabochon. Also, many which are not perfect enough for use as ornaments are utilized as bearings in watches and other precision instruments.

A few rubies of good color have been found in Macon County, North Carolina, and near Helena, Montana. But from ancient times, the mines of Upper Burma, lying east of the Irawaddy River, and about 90 miles from Mandalay, have been famous for the production of these beautiful gems. Mojok is the chief town of this ruby district. The mines were first heard of in Europe in the fifteenth century, and were mentioned by J. B. Tavernier two centuries later.

Many crudely cut rubies were set in the Burmese Royal Regalia which was transferred from the palace of the king in Mandalay in 1886 to the India Museum in London.

For centuries, these mines in Upper Burma were worked (often by prisoners); and in 1886 a company was formed called the Burma Ruby Mines which paid the government 30 per cent of its profits. Some years later the lease was surrendered because of labor and other troubles.

The rarest and most expensive ruby—often termed an "oriental ruby"—is the much prized "pigeon-blood red." Within this gem man saw "a flame everlasting and unforgettable." The finest ones of this type come from the Burma mines, not far from Mojok. Good rubies, not so dark, are mined near Bangkok; but those from Thailand (Siam) are lighter and are sometimes parti-colored.

Star rubies are extremely rare; one weighing 8 carats may cost from $1,200 to $8,000. One authority said that a fine ruby—perhaps of ten carats—sells for more than a diamond of the same weight and quality. When a star ruby is cut en cabochon, it reveals a six-rayed star of light on the summit of the stone. In 1919, a ruby of 42 carats was sold in the rough for 22,000 pounds; and a cut stone, only 7½ carats, in 1933 was valued at 10,000 pounds. Barbara Hutton, who is an inveterate collector of priceless and noted jewels, has in her possession the ruby tiara that once was worn by Empress Eugénie.

During past centuries, varied powers have been attributed to this precious stone; some considered it an antidote to poison, or believed it could protect one from the plague, banish sorrow, divert evil thoughts, and repress the bad effects of too much luxury. A ruby was said to change color if evil came near the wearer. One story has it that a ruby worn by Katherine of Aragon changed its hue when Henry VIII was considering divorcing her. Another belief was that these stones could cause water to boil.

Burmese natives thought rubies were colorless at first, and then ripened in the earth until mature. The Hindus divided them into castes; and they declared that one who possessed a high caste stone could "dwell without fear among enemies and be shielded against bad luck."

Since large rubies were uncommon, they were jealously guarded and hoarded by the rulers of Burma. However, in 1875, when one of the monarchs needed money, he sold two of the finest ones ever seen in Europe for 30,000 pounds. The best one found at Mojok was the "Nga Mauk," inherited by King Thebaw. When the British got possession of Burma, they claimed this gem as part of the regalia, but it disappeared, and has not been seen since.

Marco Polo wrote that the King of Ceylon had the finest ruby in existence, one that was large and flawless. This ruler declared that he would not part with this gem, "though all the treasures of the world were to be laid at my feet." In the former Russian Crown Jewels, there was an outstanding ruby that had been presented to Catherine the Great.

The "Timur" ruby was famous in Eastern lands for six hundred years. Weighing 352 carats, it was believed to be the largest one in the world. In 1851 the East India Company gave this gem to Queen Victoria. On it are inscriptions, both in Persian and Arabic. It was once owned by Shah Jahan, who built the incomparable Taj Mahal. The stone decorated his famous peacock throne in Delhi until the city was captured, and the Timur ruby was taken to Persia (Iran).

Another famous ruby, one of the greatest treasures in the British Crown Jewels, is the "Black Prince." It was first known in 1367, when part of the collection of the King of Granada. The Black Prince, son of Edward III, received the noted jewel as reward for the valuable aid he gave to the King of Castille at the Battle of Nagera in Northern Spain.

At the Battle of Agincourt, Henry V wore this stone in his helmet; it deflected a nearly fatal blow, and the ruby was not damaged! During Cromwell's rule, the Commonwealth ordered the crown jewels sold; however, the "Black Prince" was returned to the English authorities when Charles II came to the throne, and it was set in his crown. Today, this distinctive stone, about two inches in length and irregular in shape, has an important setting in the

Imperial Crown. A great part of its real value lies in its long connection with centuries of British history.

Often we hear stories of sunken ships, with priceless collections of jewels on board. And there is one about rubies. In 1911 the Mexican steamer, *Merida,* sank in the Chesapeake Bay, after colliding with the *Admiral Farragut.* The *Merida* took down with her a fortune in rubies alone that had belonged to Princess Carlotta of Belgium. They were stolen from her after her husband, Maximilian, had been executed. (He had been put on the throne of Mexico by Napoleon.) Later there was a revolution, and the men who had the jewels in their possession fled from the country. As far as is known, the world's most famous collection of rubies lies at the bottom of Chesapeake Bay.

In 1887 an uncut crystal of ruby, weighing 167 carats was given to the British Museum by John Ruskin in memory of Sir Herbert B. Edwardes (1819–68), "a soldier statesman in India"; this crystal was named the "Edwardes Ruby."

When abroad in 1892, Mrs. Jack Gardner of Boston, bought a famous ruby, which she wore in different ways; sometimes, as a pendant, at her waist, on her arm, or in her shoe buckle. This precious stone had been the property of an Indian Prince and was kept in the vaults of the Bank of England. When Mrs. Gardner's brother David died, she purchased the beautiful ruby, as a memorial to him, with the money he had bequeathed to her.

Although men have acclaimed this jewel as one of the most valuable items in the world, some persons of philosophical turn of mind believe other than material things to be of higher value. For instance, the Shropshire poet A. E. Housman advises:

> Give pearls away and rubies,
> But keep your fancy free.

Scripture states that "the price of wisdom is above rubies" (Job 28:18); and "wisdom is better than rubies" (Proverbs 8:11). Also in Proverbs (31:10) are these words: "Who can find a virtuous woman? For her price is far above rubies."

July Flower—Larkspur

Larkspur is "a gorgeous short-lived perennial of highly uncertain origin, but probably derived from an Asiatic group." This is an attractive garden plant of the genus Delphinium, from which many varieties are grown for their showy flowers.

The Greeks named the blossom "delphinium," because they thought the long black sepals resembled a dolphin. The name "larkspur" comes from the small sac-like petal at the back of the flower which looks like the spur of a European skylark. This flower has had various names, such as "lark's heel," "lark's toe," "lark's spur," and "knight's spur."

The larkspur or delphinium is excellent for borders, or for massing against shrubbery. The tall blue or purple spikes look well when growing against a garden wall. These lovely flowers bloom early and add much charm to spring gardens.

The hardy plant is slender, stiff and erect and sometimes grows up to a height of several feet. It has decorative leaves, and the showy flower spikes are about twelve inches long. While the predominant color of the blooms is a magnificent range of blues, including some described as "pale as the sky," "pure cobalt," or "indigo blue," there are also flowers in various shades of purple, white, yellow, pink, and rose.

In ancient days, larkspur was considered an antidote for poison. Some declared that the flower frightened away scorpions and other venomous beasts, and that they would not move until such a plant was taken away.

Larkspur was known in Britain as early as 1572, where there was a belief that its juice could strengthen and sharpen one's vision; it was also valued as a medicine to heal wounds. One variety, quite different from the garden type, reached the British Isles and was known as "wilde larke spur."

By 1629, there were in England both single and double kinds of this flower in varied shades. It is not known when the first real delphinium (the glorious perennial relative of the larkspur) was developed. In 1859, when the firm of James Kelway was specializing in them, progress became rapid. By the end of the century it is reported that 137 types had been developed in England, Holland, and the United States.

According to one source there are 150 species of this plant, with about sixty growing in North America. Larkspurs flourish in many parts of the Temperate Zone, from Tibet to California; they are seen in various sections of Europe, blooming in fields, and making roadsides attractive.

One tall wild variety grows from western Pennsylvania to the Carolinas and Alabama and on to Nebraska. In the U.S.A. there are many native larkspurs, some of which are found on the Pacific Coast from Southern California north to Washington. The best loved delphinium is the "Colorado," grown westward from the plains, and northward even as far as Alaska. This popular plant has clear sky-blue color, with pale yellow upper petals.

Alternate July Flower—Water Lily

> O star on the breast of the river!
> O marvel of bloom and grace!

The water lily is also a July flower, and it is surely one of the most beautiful. The name "water lily" is given to various aquatic perennials that are rooted in mud. There are about forty distinct species and many varieties. These flowers are cultivated in the warmer parts of the world, and have been popular since ancient times in India, China, Japan, Persia, and other eastern countries. Early Teutons used this plant as an ornament and in their heraldry.

On the North American continent such plants are in bloom from June to September, from Nova Scotia to the Gulf of Mexico, and west to the Mississippi. The yellow pond lily, called "cow lily" or "frog lily," blooms all summer from Labrador to the Rockies, and south to Texas and Florida.

Some water lilies are day bloomers, others open at night; the hardy kinds are cultivated as perennials, and may be pure white, red, or bronze and copper-colored. Tropical lilies are annuals and are showier than the hardy ones. Their blooms are mostly blue, purple, or pink, but lack the yellow tints of the hardy species.

Water lilies are anchored by thick stems to the rich mud of ponds, lakes or the bottoms of slowly moving streams. The waxy leaves may be oval, round, or heart-shaped. The conspicuously attractive flowers rise singly on long stems, and float on the smooth surface of the water. Helen Hunt Jackson has given us a beautiful picture of these blossoms:

> The white heat pales the skies from side to side;
> But in still lakes and rivers, cool, content,
> Like starry flowers on a new firmament,
> White lilies float and regally abide.

In May, the leaves appear; then in June, the buds; and when the days are longer and warmer, each flower, "a radiant, floating cup," rises and falls with the water. The blossom, from four to eight inches across, opens about 6 A.M., and closes at night. The life of the bloom is about three days. Besides growing wild, many water lilies are cultivated in garden pools for their fragrance that attracts bees and birds.

These flowers vary much in size; the largest and most noted species is the annual, "Victoria Regia," native to Guiana and Brazil. (It is also found on tropical islands—on Mauretius in the Indian Ocean, for example—where some wonderful specimens can be seen.) Victoria Regia is also grown in the hothouses of great botanical gardens like those at Kew, not far from London. The leaves, from 4 to 6 feet in diameter, turn up at the edges, and are prickly underneath. The rose-white flowers are from 12 to 18 inches in width. It is reported that when they are growing, they expand at the rate of one inch per hour. In South America the seeds of the Victoria Regia are collected for food.

In 1850 Jane Loudon, the "lady" gardener and writer on gardening, stopped at Chatsworth, the home of the Paxton family. There she saw for the first time (in the huge glass house that contained "the treasured darling" of Mr. Paxton's heart) the fabulous Amazon water lily, named "Victoria Regia" for the Queen. She came to "an amazed standstill" for

Here was the flower which had become the talk of the nation. It floated in proud isolation on the water. A mammoth bloom of wax-white, curvaceous petals. But the water-lily, beautiful and strange though it was, did not seem nearly so remarkable to Jane as its leaves. She was astonished by their extraordinary size and shape. They lay spread on the water like gigantic green platters . . . measuring some five feet ten inches in diameter . . .

When you think of water lilies, you are reminded of a beautiful scene which one writer has described in this fashion:

Then floating about in a birch canoe, among the lily pads, while one envies the moose and deer that feed on fare so dainty and spend their lives around scenes of such exquisite beauty, one lets thoughts also float as idly as the little clouds high overhead.

While poets and prose writers have paid tribute to the beauty of the water lily, artists have also made it the subject of paintings.

Chief among the masters who have depicted this flower is Claude Monet, the noted French Impressionist. For years his work was scorned; salons did not permit his paintings to be hung; and he worked in abject poverty. Finally his genius was recognized; and by 1874, he was a leader of the Impressionists. One writer wrote of his works:

Seen close up, his pictures were a preposterous hodgepodge of colored dabs and dashes; viewed from a distance, they trembled with life and irridescence.

In 1890, Monet bought a farmhouse at Giverny, and created a pond, 100 by 300 feet. By diverting a small stream, he had a continual flow of water through the pool. He had gardeners plant different kinds of water lilies in this pond, and at one end, the artist built a Japanese footbridge.

It is said that Monet would stand for hours at a time on this bridge, watching the delicate water lilies as they floated on the

surface. He would go there early in the morning to watch them
open their petals and return at night to see them close.

From this vantage point, the artist studied the reflections of sky
and clouds, at different hours and seasons, on bright or overcast
days, when winds "scudded" the clouds, and when there was no
breeze. Here is how Monet describes what he saw:

Upon the saturated greens, blues, siennas, and ochres of the pool and its
wavering reflections, the lily pads and blossoms, viewed in recession, lie
like a rich but tattered carpet with threads of pink and white.

Monet's water garden with its lilies inspired many of his pictures
and gave him a rich harvest of paintings. He once said, "These
landscapes of water and reflections have become an obsession with
me." Between 1904 and 1908 he did 48 canvases on this one subject.
These were hung at the noted Durand-Ruel Gallery in Paris.

In 1916, with failing eyesight, the painter entered upon the most
ambitious project of his entire life. For this, he built a studio 70 by
40 feet, and 50 feet high. He ordered fifty 7 by 15 foot canvases.

After he had begun to paint his water lilies, he often became
discouraged and said in despair: "I have undertaken things impossible to execute. . . . One can go crazy trying to paint them. . . .
It is beyond the strength of an old man."

Monet really tortured himself in this project; often he would
destroy works that didn't please him. But he continued, hoping that
something worthwhile would come out of this effort.

In 1918, the day after the Armistice, Premier Georges Clemenceau came to his studio. He urged the artist to give these water lily
paintings to France to commemorate the victory of World War I.
Monet consented on these terms: the works should be housed in a
suitable building, and he should be allowed to revise them as much
as he wished.

For several years he worked on endlessly repainting. One day
when he was eighty-two years of age, he took Clemenceau into the
studio and the report is that the Premier "was staggered by the
loveliness of what he saw."

After Claude Monet's death, in accordance with his wishes, his immense landscapes—Les Nympheas (water lilies) reaching about 300 feet in length—were placed in the Musée de l'Orangerie in Paris, where "they are a monument to a genius so stubborn, yet so lyrical that it could transform a pond into a timeless mirage."

Other water lily paintings by Monet can be seen in various European galleries, including the Buhrle Collection in Zurich, Switzerland, and the Granoff, in Paris. In the United States one— 6½ by 42 feet—hangs in the Museum of Modern Art in New York; another (78 by 234 inches) is in the collection of Walter P. Chrysler, Jr., in New York; and another Monet water lily work is at the Boston Museum of Fine Arts.

So the showy water lily has been highly honored by this distinguished French painter, and its beauty depicted for all to see and admire.

Stories and legends have become attached to the water lily too; one German fable relates that the water nymphs would hide from men by changing into water lilies, then resume their shapes when the strangers had passed by. In primitive days these flowers were also a symbol of purity as attested by the following:

This flower, rising through pure water, and unfolding to the sun in petals of snow, has been fitly chosen to represent chastity . . .

Often water lilies were carried at funerals before the bier of the deceased as emblematic of his virtue. The plants were known as far back as Pliny; they were thought to be protection against witches, and able to break an enchantment—except for the most powerful ones.

In the United States there is a legend about an Indian maiden who loved a certain warrior. However, her parents had promised her to another and she obediently tried to avoid the man she loved. One day he followed her and tried to embrace her, but the girl eluded him, ran up a steep rock by the river, and warned him not to pursue her. When he persisted, she dived into the water and disappeared. The following day the Indians were surprised to find a water lily growing at the spot. Their prophet explained to them that the lovely maid had become this beautiful flower forever.

From Paolo Mantegazza, an Italian physiologist and anthropologist, comes this story of some especially fine roses that grew in a garden high on a cliff: A young girl had refused some roses her youth had offered her, wanting only the white ones growing on the rock. To please her he tried to scale the dangerous cliff, but she pleaded for him to return. Asked what his reward would be if he succeeded in his perilous mission, the girl promised him her "whole heart." Frightened, she looked on while he plucked the roses with one hand as he held on to the cliff with the other. Suddenly the roses fell into the stream, and the young lover after them. Luckily, he escaped with his life, but the girl laughed at him for getting a ducking and refused his love. At this point the rose petals floating on the water also became disillusioned and changed into water lilies.

William Hone, in his *Mirror of Months*, gives an unforgettable description of the water lily in its native habitat:

Now, if we pass near some gently lapsing water, we may chance to meet with the splendid flowers of the great water lily floating on the surface of the stream, like some fairy vessel at anchor. . . . Nothing can be more elegant than each of the three different states under which this flower now appears: the first, while it lies unopened among its undulating leaves, like the halcyon's egg within its floating nest; next when its snowy petals are but half expanded, and you are almost tempted to wonder what beautiful bird it is that has just taken its flight from such a sweet birthplace; and lastly when the whole flower floats confessed, and spreading wide upon the water its pointed petals, offers its whole heart to the enamoured sun . . .

August

The eighth was August, being richly arrayed,
In garments all of gold, down to the ground . . .
—EDMUND SPENSER

OUR eighth month, August, once called "the forerunner of splendid beauties" was originally named "Sextilis" by the Romans, as it was the sixth in their calendar. At first August had 29 days, then, for some time, 30.

Julius Caesar had adopted his nephew, Gaius Julius Caesar Octavianus, and made him his heir. The Senate gave this ruler the title of "Augustus," meaning "revered" or "reverend." (Later emperors added this to their names.)

The Senate honored Augustus by naming a month for him. Although he had been born in September, he did not choose that month, but preferred Sextilis. For during it, many fortunate events had happened to him: the celebration of three triumphs; his admission to the Consulate; the conquest of Egypt; the Roman soldiers pledging their allegiance to him at the Janiculum; and the cessation of all civil wars. Therefore, "Sextilis" became "August"; and the Emperor took one day from February, adding it to August, so that his month would have thirty-one days, the same as July that honored his uncle, Julius Caesar.

Anglo-Saxons termed August "Arn-monath" ("arn" meaning "harvest"); for at that time they were busily filling their barns with the harvested crops. Since the hot weather continued during the month, everything grew rapidly; weeds were plentiful; so the Saxons also called this time "Weod-monath."

In her poem, "August," Helen Hunt Jackson wrote:

> Pathetic summer seeks by blazonry
> Of color to conceal her swift decrease . . .
> Poor middle-aged summer! Vain this show!
> Whole fields of goldenrod cannot offset
> One meadow with a single violet . . .

When the crops were being gathered, rural districts in England presented busy scenes, and these were favorite subjects for early writers. In Hone, for example, we find this stanza:

> See the reapers dining
> Seated on the shady grass;
> O'er the gate the squire reclining,
> Slily eyes each ruddy lass.

And that prolific poet, John Clare, in his *Shepherd's Calendar* has given us an excellent picture of the August countryside:

> The fields are all alive with sultry noise,
> Of labor's sounds, and insects' busy joys;
> The reapers o'er their glittering sickles stoop,
> Startling full oft the partridge coveys up;
> Some o'er the rustling scythe go bending
> And shockers follow where their traces have gone,
> Heaping the swaths that rustle in the sun.

The most popular holiday of the entire year, in England, the much welcomed "Harvest Home" was celebrated in August; and Leigh Hunt commented as follows:

This is the month of harvest . . . Harvest Home is still the greatest rural holiday in England because it concludes at once the most laborious and most lucrative of the farmer's employments, and unites repose and profit.

A writer named Stevenson, in 1661, in his *Twelve Moneth*
mentions the fact that in this month of August

The furmenty pot welcomes home the harvest cart, and the garland of
flowers crowns the captain of the reapers. . . . O, 'tis a merry time
wherein harvest neighbors make good cheer; and God is glorified in His
blessings on the earth.

After the last wagon had carried its load to the barn, the land-
owner and his workers gathered for a festive meal. This was often
spread in the barn, where all rejoiced together over the bountiful
harvest. Such a scene has been well described by an early poet:

> The ears are filled, the fields are white,
> The constant harvest moon is bright
> To grasp the bounty of the year.
> The reapers to the scene repair. . . .
> The meals are done as soon as tasted
> And neither time nor viands wasted,
> All over—then the barrels foam—
> The "largess-cry," the "Harvest Home."

August has furnished diverse celebrities to the world, including
three United States Presidents: Benjamin Harrison, Herbert Hoover
and Lyndon B. Johnson. Other notables are Thomas Gainsborough,
Percy B. Shelley, Harry Lauder, Alfred Tennyson, Princess Margaret, Carrie Jacobs Bond, Annie Oakley, Leo Tolstoy, Napoleon,
Sir Walter Scott, Princess Anne, Frederick the Great, and Bernard
M. Baruch.

Still others include Prince Albert, Queen Wilhelmina, Dorothy
Parker, Alonzo Stagg, Franz Hals, Izaak Walton, Goethe, Orville
Wright, Maeterlinck, Davy Crockett, Marshall Field, and Billie
Burke.

The following are some of the many historic events that have
occurred during the month of August: in 1456 the Gutenberg Bible
was completed; in 1501, Columbus first landed on the continent of
North America; in 1588 the Spanish Armada went down in defeat;

in 1642 there was the first commencement at Harvard; in 1770 Captain James Cook took possession of Australia for England; in 1789 the U.S. War Department was organized; in 1790 the first national American census was taken; and in 1831 the first steam railroad went into operation.

In 1806 the first coal was mined in the United States; in 1807 the Steamer *Clermont* sailed on the Hudson River; in 1814 Dolly Madison fled from the burning White House; in 1846 the Smithsonian Institution was established; in 1851 the U.S.A. won the first yacht race with England; in 1857, the first express office was opened—in Omaha, Nebraska; in 1859 oil was discovered at Titusville, Pennsylvania; in 1884 the cornerstone for the Statue of Liberty was laid; and in 1896 the Alaska Gold Rush was on.

In the year 1920 the 19th Amendment to the Constitution went into effect, giving the women of America the right to vote; in 1926 Gertrude Ederle swam the English Channel; in 1927 the U.S.-Canadian Peace Bridge was opened; in 1928 the Kellog Peace Treaty was signed; in 1934 Adolf Hitler took over Germany; in 1935 Will Rogers and Wiley Post lost their lives in an aeroplane crash; in 1944 the Allies liberated Paris; in 1945 General McArthur landed in Japan; that same year the first atomic bomb was dropped on Hiroshima; in 1954 one of the Dionne Quintuplets—Emilie—died; and in 1958 the *Nautilus*, a nuclear-powered submarine, made the first undersea crossing at the North Pole.

During August there are several dates worthy of remembrance. For example, August 4 is observed in some places as U.S. Coast Guard Day, which traces its beginning to the founding of the U.S. Revenue Marine, on August 4, 1790.

Also it is well to recall that on August 14, 1941, the results of an official meeting of Winston Churchill and Franklin D. Roosevelt were made public. The document the meeting produced—the Atlantic Charter—revealed the peace aims of the United States and Great Britain, and the sincere desire of the two nations for world disarmament. Four years later, on the same date, August 14 (1945) came the welcome Victory of V-J Day, when Japan surrendered.

August Birthstone—Sardonyx

The August birthstone, the sardonyx, is a kind of onyx, which contains layers of sard, a brownish-red variety of chalcedony classed by some as a variety of carnelian. Sard got its name from Sardes, capital of Lydia. (Chalcedony is a quartz with a waxy lustre, that comes in various colors and forms.)

Often in sardonyx there is a white layer contrasting with the brownish-red one; this latter color is caused by the presence of iron oxide. This is the only kind of chalcedony that has commercial value, and it is found in different parts of the world. Sometimes the stripes can be easily seen in the sardonyx; in others, only through a microscope. It is reported that once Sir David Brewster found a sardonyx that had 17,000 bands in one inch. Sometimes such stones have been discovered with natural designs in them.

From early times good specimens of sardonyx have been found in India. Both the Greeks and Romans used black and white onyx and sardonyx in making cameos of fine quality, also intaglios. In the past many attractive objects of art, such as boxes and vases, have been made from these stones.

As with other gems, some medicinal qualities became associated with them. Pliny wrote that certain varieties were good to use on wounds that had been inflicted by scorpions or spiders, and that such stones from India had "great and marvelous properties."

Alternate August Birthstone—Peridot (Olivine)

The alternate August birthstone, the peridot (or olivine), is a semi-precious gem, a variety of chrysolite. The most desired kind is the true bottle green color in varying depths; others are found in a darker olive green, yellowish-green, or yellowish-brown.

This really beautiful green gem is much desired for jewelry.

However, the stones vary in substance; many are relatively soft, and their use in rings is not encouraged. But some, because of their pleasing hues, are used for this purpose.

The French call this stone "peridot" (although the name is not believed to be of French origin). The term "olivine" is preferred by many. It was applied to the gem in 1790 by A. J. Warner, and is in common use by English and German mineralogists.

Peridots have been found in many localities, including Queensland, in Australia; Norway; Minas Gerais, in Brazil; the Belgian Congo; Upper Burma; South Africa; and on the beaches of Hawaii. In the United States, some bright green grains of olivine have been discovered in Arizona and New Mexico where they have been known locally as "Job's tears."

The finest specimens have come mainly from an island, Zebirget (St. John's), on the western side of the Red Sea, about fifty miles from the Egyptian port of Berenice. Magnficent, clear, rich, green gems, called "Levantine peridots" have been found there, of sufficient size to make them very valuable. Some have weighed as much as 80 carats. These well guarded mines were once the monopoly of the Khedive of Egypt, but they were closed in 1914.

In recent years some exceptionally fine peridots were discovered in a house in Alexandria, Egypt. It is not known whether they were connected with a theft, or were kept there because of some superstition.

The outstanding example of the peridot is one that was part of the Russian Crown Jewels. This gem, olive green in color, was an almost perfect oblong and weighed over 192 carats. Originally, it was set in a distinctive mounting, and was surrounded by 30 brilliants. Other peridots of high quality have been used in ecclesiastical jewelry.

One authority declares that this gem with "its rich and constant unmistakable color" (it has often been called the "evening emerald") has not yet attained the popularity its beauty rightly deserves. However, peridots are becoming better known and liked; and since their number is limited, the demand may exceed the meagre supply.

August Flower—Poppy

> But pleasures are like poppies spread,
> You seize the flower, its bloom is dead.
> —ROBERT BURNS

The August flower, the poppy, called a flower of "sleep and oblivion," is any species of the genus Papaver. This name comes from the Latin, "papaver" from the same root as "pap." The Saxon word for this plant was "popig." According to some sources, there are more than a hundred species of poppies.

The poppy has been known from antiquity. It is "a bristly, hairy herb," bearing delicate, brilliant flowers with long, silky, almost transparent petals. The hardy plant comes in several varieties, and in midsummer adds much color to gardens and fields. It has long been a favorite of artists; early Dutch painters often included these flowers in their works.

There are several different kinds of poppies, but the striking Eastern or Oriental poppy is considered the best. It is believed to have originated in the remote valleys where Persia and Afghanistan meet. (Later a blood-red type was brought from Siberia.)

The Oriental poppy has huge bisected, hairy leaves, often up to 18 inches long and clumps of luxuriant foliage. Its orange-scarlet bloom carries an atmosphere of exotic splendor with it. This type of poppy has been cultivated extensively in gardens all over the world. However, it is not good for use as a cut flower indoors, as it withers very quickly.

Recently an authority stated that the present-day Oriental poppies "with their advanced ruffling and bright new colorings, should not be overlooked on the 'most wanted' list of perennials for fall planting."

The Walter Marx Gardens of Boring, Oregon, have vastly enlarged the selection of this type of flower. They have produced edged bicolors, fully double varieties, of new, and also of blended shades. Careful breeding, too, has produced poppies that are from 8 to 12 inches across, yielding a bright display through May and June.

The ordinary scarlet or "corn poppy" has long adorned the countryside of Continental Europe and the British Isles. They often grow wild in wheat and hay fields. Since the plant is hard to get rid of, farmers sometimes call it "redweed," "canker," or "headache." Of this flower Helen Hunt Jackson has written:

> The poppies, lithe and fleet
> Seem running fiery torchmen, to and fro
> To mark the shore. . . .
> I shall be glad remembering how the fleet,
> Lithe poppies run like torchmen through the wheat.

Another poppy is the "Shirley," named for a small town in Surrey, England, where the Rev. Mr. Wilks began to grow them in 1880. The "Iceland" is a native of the far northern regions of Siberia, Iceland, and Canada. In their wild state these plants produced yellow flowers that were good for indoor use; but under cultivation, other colors have been developed.

The red variety of this plant is not native to the United States, but the California poppy, "Eschscholtzia," is; and so it was chosen for the state flower. When the Spanish explorers arrived on the Pacific Coast, the poppies were in bloom; in fact, it is said that they formed "a blanket of gold from the foothills to the sea." Each flower was "a cup of gold," while the great expanse of poppies was named the "altar cloth of San Pascual." Therefore, the newcomers called this region "the Land of Fire," and the "Golden West." And no one who has ever seen a field of California poppies in full bloom can forget the beautiful sight.

Now the California poppy is grown all over the world, in many gardens. When an English ship cruised along the Pacific Coast in 1792, Archibald Menzies gathered some of these poppy seeds and gave them to the famous Kew Botanical Gardens, near London. After growing there for some time they were lost, then re-discovered in 1815, by Chamisso. He was a member of Captain Kotzebue's expedition to the West Coast; and he complimented a friend and fellow voyager, Dr. Johann Eschscholtz, by naming the California poppy "Eschscholtzia Californica," for him.

Luther Burbank developed several varieties, in different shades, of this showy flower, which has "feathery, dusty green leaves." Its flowers—from 3 to 4 inches across—grow singly on long stalks. One admirer calls it "the prettiest and gayest of annuals."

The oldest known type of poppy—and the most important—is the opium poppy, a native of the Middle East, where it grew wild around the Mediterranean. For centuries before the Christian era, these plants were cultivated by the Greeks, Romans, Egyptians, and other peoples who made opium from the silky latex that appeared when any part of the plant was scratched. For many years the process was kept secret, and the manufacture of opium was confined mostly to Persia and Asia Minor.

It seems that from primitive times people knew of the narcotic and soporific effects of opium. They used it to soothe headaches and to induce sleep. Sometimes poppy seeds, or their juice, was added to babies' foods to help them go to sleep. In the early nineteenth century a concoction called "Godfrey's Cordial" was given to quiet children; some adults also sampled it and found that it contained a good deal of opium.

At first, Europeans imported opium from the East, but later poppies were cultivated extensively in other places. It is said that one acre of them could produce fifty-six pounds of opium. Some of the familiar drugs containing opium are laudanum, morphine, and codeine. Several important literary figures, including George Crabbe, Samuel T. Coleridge, Thomas de Quincy, and Francis Thompson, used laudanum as "an inducer of delicious delirium."

The making of opium played an important part in the history of the East. For centuries poppies had been grown and opium processed in India; then the drug was smuggled into China. It is reported that the East India Company "kept its skirts clean, by having no official connection with the traffic."

Great Britain wanted China to open its doors to commercial trade, but the latter refused. When some warships accompanied opium vessels to China, the Chinese fired on them and the "Opium War" (November, 1839–August, 1842) was on. It ended with the surrender of China; this country then ceded Hong Kong to the British and opened five ports. One source states that since opium was still contraband, the drug was not mentioned, and the illegal traffic went on until 1908. This "Opium War" was frowned upon by many of the British. Prime Minister William Gladstone had the moral courage to vote for "censure." He deplored the fact that the British Flag had become "a pirate flag to protect an infamous traffic."

Today governments are still struggling against this business; and "the illicit poppy fruit" still makes news. Robert Wilder, a novelist of Southern California, has recently written a book, *Fruit of the Poppy*. It is the story of the opium poppy, which some Chinese colonists about two hundred years ago taught native Mexicans to grow.

The job of stamping out the illegal business is a difficult one on both sides of the border. The Mexicans are deeply concerned about this traffic and are ashamed of it. They have outlawed the growing of the poppy, and go into the districts with planes from which they burn the fields, unfortunately sometimes setting fire to villages and good timberlands.

When they send troops to destroy the fields, natives often jump out from ambush and kill some of the soldiers.

Peon farmers grow the poppies in hidden valleys, often high up in the mountains of Sinaloa, Sonora, Chihuahua, and Durango. They have to build fences of cacti around the poppy fields because cattle love to eat the pods; and the result has been many "hopped up" animals. The growers sell the "gum" to itinerant peddlers.

Even though these law-breakers know they are working illegally, they keep on growing the poppies because of the fantastic profits. It is said that one small field will yield opium to the value of $10,000. After this amount has been transformed into morphine, then into heroin, it has a value of about $100,000.

In 1965 the Chief of the Judiciary Police in Mexico City reported that about 600 fields had been destroyed. The United States has been helping the Mexican government in the fight against this traffic by supplying planes, helicopters, flame throwers, rifles, and other needed equipment.

Not long ago the Collector of Customs at San Diego reported that in one year three times as much narcotics had been seized in this district as in any other in the U.S.—narcotics that would bring about $7,000,000 on the illegal market!

And the writer, Robert Wilder, has stated in regard to the illicit trade:

The job of stamping it out is enormous on both sides of the border; and there's a constant trickle from Mexico to the United States. Our Bureau of Narcotics is undermanned and can't possibly police the border from Brownsville to San Ysidro. In summer the Rio Grande dries up and there's nothing to prevent a man from walking across there.

In contrast to the harmful use of the poppy, France extracts a valuable oil from the seeds and uses it as a substitute for olive oil. The seeds are also used in cooking and sprinkled on rolls and cakes. They also serve as food for birds, and furnish a drying oil for artists.

One classic myth relates that after Pluto had carried Proserpina off, her mother, Ceres, cried to the other gods for help in finding her daughter. They were not able to aid her; so Somnus, the god of sleep, created poppies around the place where Ceres had sat down to rest. She picked and ate some of the juicy seeds, yielded to their soothing influence; and so "was lost to all sadness and despair in blessed oblivion." After her refreshing sleep, she went back to the grain she had neglected, and at once the crops revived. This goddess is often shown with poppies and corn in her hair.

Poppies in early times were offered to the dead, so they became a symbol of death and were considered plants of bad omen. When the son of Tarquinius Superbus asked him what should be done with the inhabitants of a conquered city, Tarquinius went into his garden. There he slashed off the heads of the largest poppies, and thus recommended the deaths of the most influential citizens of the town. Another legend tells that after a maid had gone out and slain a great dragon, poppies grew from the spots where the monster's blood had fallen.

Several stories have arisen from the fact that early peoples believed poppies often grew on battlefields from the blood of slain soldiers. In Holland, after the Battle of Neerwinden, the fields became covered with poppies. The belief was that these were the blood of 20,000 men, and a sign that Heaven was angry because of men's evil deeds.

There have been several poets who have sung about these flowers, including John Keats, who described someone as:

> . . . sound asleep
> Drowsed with the fume of poppies.

The Quaker poet, John Greenleaf Whittier, also referred to this plant:

> . . . to eat the lotus of the Nile,
> And drink the poppies of Cathay.

No doubt the well-known poem, "In Flanders Fields" which begins with the lines:

> In Flanders Fields the poppies blow
> Between the crosses, row on row . . .

will be longest remembered for its connection with poppies. This is considered by many "the greatest poem in English occasioned by World War I." It was written in 1915 by Colonel John McCrae, a Canadian medical officer, during a lull in the Second Battle of Ypres. He wrote it on a sheet torn from a dispatch book, and *Punch* published it anonymously.

Each year, "Poppy Day" is observed on the Saturday nearest November 11—the former Armistice Day, now Veterans Day—when red crepe paper poppies are sold for war charities. The first time poppies were worn to honor the war dead occurred in New York on November 9, 1918. The custom was started by Miss Meina Michael of Georgia. Paper poppies were first sold publicly on the streets of Milwaukee, Wisconsin, through the efforts of Mrs. Mary Hanecy of that city, in June, 1919.

Today, many of the paper poppies are made by patients in

Veterans' Hospitals. For example, for the May 1966 sales in Los Angeles and Orange Counties in Southern California, more than 63,000 were produced; one young veteran—a bed patient—made 8,500 of these Memorial Day mementos.

These men are paid for their work, and in some cases, it is their only means of support. The American Legion units buy them at four cents each, and their volunteer workers sell them on the streets. The revenue from this project is used for "child welfare, and for rehabilitation of veterans and their families."

Alternate August Flower—Gladiolus

The alternate August flower—the gladiolus—is now claimed by some to be the most widely cultivated and most extensively used of all plants. According to an expert, Joe Littlefield, "the preferred pronunciation is 'glad-DIE-o-lus,' whereas the popular usage is 'glad-di-O-lus,' the nickname 'glads.' "

The flowers are easy to grow; they look beautiful in gardens—especially when planted in masses; they are excellent for house use. In short, the gladiolus is "one of the most popular of all cut flowers that can be raised by both amateurs and professionals."

This plant, "a lily-like member of the iris family," is a stately and effective garden flower; there are said to be more than 250 species in different countries. Although a native of South Africa, it has now become a truly "world flower." French and Dutch gardeners improved the plants and produced numerous hybrids. The modern varieties are larger and much more attractive than their ancestors. And "grace of form and beauty of bloom distinguish the gladiolus." One especially fine type came from the region near famous Victoria Falls, and was first shown at a horticultural show in 1904.

Another species, the "gladiolus tristis" from South Africa, has a delightful fragrance noticeable only in the evening. This type is not so tall or robust as some others; it has "yellowish-white, purple-streaked, night-blooming flowers that suggest the tuberose in sweetness."

The "Gardening Lady," Jane Loudon, was fond of gladioli, and in one of her books (written in the 19th century), *Ornamental Bulbous Plants*, she spoke highly of the "Changeable Gladiolus":

. . . the colours of whose petals at sunset take a curiously shifting hue like that of shot-silk when held up to the light.

Mrs. Loudon recommended that this gladiolus was well suited for growing in a box on a veranda where the rays of the setting sun could reach it. She also declared: "It is sweeter smelling by far at dusk."

Another type which this discriminating gardener admired was the "Viper Gladiolus." Its greenish-grey petals were "marked by livid brown stripes" that looked like "the head of a viper, when held erect and ready to strike." Despite the evil look, Jane Loudon recommended this type of gladiolus for its delicious scent. "Viper Gladiolus" was first introduced into England in 1794, was lost for some time, and then rediscovered in 1825.

The word "gladiolus," meaning "small sword," was chosen because its long leaves are shaped like swords. The term comes from the Latin, *gladius*, denoting "sword." During the sixteenth century, this flower was known as "sword-flag"; other European names for it include "sword-lily" and "corn-flag."

During the Middle Ages one writer declared that a poultice made from gladiolus roots would draw out a thorn or splinter; also that colic pains could be relieved by a mixture of goat's milk and gladiolus roots.

The blossoms of this distinctive plant are funnel-shaped and grow on sturdy stems. The flowers begin to unfold at the base and then extend their openings to the top. Gladioli are very popular as home decorations, and come in such hues as orchid, pink, violet, maroon, red, yellow, white, or salmon. Some are grown from seeds, others from bulbs; and they can easily be killed by frost.

Since this plant was introduced into the United States, about the middle of the nineteenth century, countless types have been developed in this country. Florida is reported to be the leading state in supplying such flowers for the northern winter market.

The All-American Gladiolus Selections group maintains forty-six gardens in the U.S.A. and Canada, where the flowers are raised in many kinds of soil and climates. The choices for 1961 were "Rusty," "Gypsy Dancer," and "China Blue." (Since the first All-America award, only twelve out of hundreds have earned this top rating.)

Rusty is the first All-American "smoky"—massive, but well proportioned; Gypsy Dancer symbolizes "a care-free dancing mood," has a "fresh, vibrant color"; while China Blue is soft-blue-violet, and is "a robust grower."

In 1962 at the climax of the gladiolus season in London, several resplendent collections were shown at the New Horticultural Hall in Westminster, at the Royal Horticultural Society's show. Several new varieties were displayed, including "K.M.'s Blue"—a deep violet shade; a vivid type called "Gypsy Love"; "Magic Beauty," with subtle coloring; and "Blue Haze."

While the gladiolus is raised in many countries and used extensively for decorative purposes, the world's largest gladiolus farms are in Southern California, between Los Angeles and San Diego, not far from the town of Carlsbad.

For a few weeks in late spring or early summer these farms offer a rainbow spectacle. They are owned by Edwin Frazee, the world's largest shipper of gladiolus. They are cut and shipped regularly up to Memorial Day. Recently the owner sent out 135,000 dozen in a two-week period.

After Memorial Day, the harvest slows down, but until late in June the fields are usually in brilliant bloom. Many visitors drive down past the great Marine Base of Camp Pendleton, on to Oceanside and Carlsbad. A few miles farther on, one leaves the freeway and reaches the farms. This is an unusually fine spectacle; for on the hundred acres it is a real thrill to see these beautiful "glads" in every hue of the rainbow.

September

The golden rod is yellow,
The corn is turning brown,
The trees in apple orchards
With fruit are bending down . . .
By all these lovely tokens
September days are here,
With summer's best of weather
And autumn's best of cheer.
—HELEN HUNT JACKSON

SEPTEMBER, our ninth month, was the seventh in the Roman calendar. In spite of attempts by the Senate, the Romans did not change the names of the last four months of the year: September (seventh), October (eighth), November (ninth), and December (tenth). Yet, after they had added the months of January and February, these four monthly terms were no longer correct or fitting.

The word "September" stems from the Latin *septem*, meaning "seven." During this period, the Romans celebrated some important games, the Ludi Magni (beginning on September 4), honoring the king of the gods Jupiter, Juno, and Minerva. When Julius Caesar reformed the calendar, he gave September an additional day, making it 31. Later this day was removed; hence, "Thirty days hath September. . . ."

In the time of Charlemagne, this month was called "Harvest Month." The Anglo-Saxons named it "Gerst-monath" or "Barley month," during which they harvested the barley and made their brew. They also used the name "Holy Month" for September because at that time they ovserved an ancient religious festival. In Switzerland this month is still called "Harvest Month."

September has always been associated with the gathering of crops and agricultural fairs, with fine displays of grains, fruits, vegetables, live stock, and many things of general interest to farmers and their families.

In an interesting old English book, *The Mirror of Months*, is this picture of September:

. . . the fruit garden is one scene of tempting profusion. Against the wall, the grapes have put on that transparent look, which indicates their complete ripeness. . . . The peaches and nectarines have become frag-rant. . . . the rosy-cheeked apples look out from among their leaves, like laughing children peeping at each other through screens of foliage.

And Leigh Hunt writes of this time of the year:

This is the month of the migration of birds, of the finished harvest, of nut-gatherings, of cyder making, and towards the conclusion, of the change of color in trees . . . Its noblest nature is a certain festive abundance for the supply of all creation.

In September, the moon is high above the horizon, and furnishes light for workers to continue their labors late in the fields. This moon has often been hailed, and sung about, as the "harvest moon." Other natural aspects also make this season memorable:

> Yet still shall sage September boast his pride,
> Some birds shall chant, some gayer flowers shall blow.

The autumn equinox occurs during this time of year. Usually, the weather is pleasant, even though mornings and nights are often chilly. Storms may come; so farmers are busily engaged storing their products in barns before the autumn rains fall.

Soon as the sun is off the ground,
Rumblings like distant thunder sound.
The waggons haste the corn to load,
And hurry down the dusty road.
—JOHN CLARE, in *The Shepherd's Calendar*

The harvest men sung summer out
With thankful song, and joyous shout;
And when September comes, they hail
The autumn with the flapping flail . . .

During this ninth month, only one President had his birthday—William Howard Taft, born in 1857. Other important individuals born in September were Rex Beach, Eugene Field, Cardinal Richelieu, Elizabeth I, Grandma Moses, O. Henry, Michael Faraday, Henry Hudson, General Pershing, Tintoretto, Alexander the Great, William McGuffey (compiler of the old readers), and George Gershwin.

Others with September birthdays were Samuel Adams, Frances E. Willard, Lord Nelson, Kate Douglas Wiggin, Upton Sinclair, Greta Garbo, Lafayette, Richard the Lion-hearted, Hamlin Garland, Dr. Samuel Johnson, Walter Pidgeon, and Jane Addams.

During past centuries distinctive happenings have taken place during September; for examples, in 1666 the Great Fire started in London; in 1774 the first Continental Congress was in session; in 1776 Nathan Hale was captured; in 1781 the pueblo of Los Angeles was founded; in 1784 the United States had its first daily newspaper; in 1787 the U.S. Constitution was signed; in 1789 the U.S. Supreme Court was founded, Alexander Hamilton became the first Secretary of the Treasury, and the U.S. Treasury was organized.

In 1793 the cornerstone of the National Capitol was laid; in 1796 President George Washington made his famous Farewell Address; in 1797 the *Constitution* (Old Ironsides) was launched; in 1830 the first balloon ascension occurred in America; in 1846 Elias Howe invented the sewing machine; in 1850 the Swedish singer, Jenny Lind, arrived in New York City; in 1851 the first edition of the *New York Times* appeared; in 1864 Atlanta, Georgia, was captured by the Union forces; and in 1882 the first Labor Day was celebrated in America.

In 1898 radium was discovered; in 1901 President William Mc-Kinley was shot at Buffalo; in 1908 Orville Wright stayed in the air more than an hour in his flying machine; in 1916 the first armored tank was used on a battlefield; in 1927 Babe Ruth made his sixtieth home run; in 1937, Germany invaded Poland; and in 1937 the Munich Pact was signed.

Some important holidays are observed in the United States during September. Labor Day, which falls on the first Monday in the month, is devoted to honoring the importance and dignity of work, and all laboring people. The weekend on which it occurs has become a major holiday, and officially ends the summer season.

Citizenship Day, on September 17, was formerly termed Constitution Day, because our national body of laws was ratified on that day in 1787. At first this holiday was celebrated to call attention to the greatness and the wise provisions of our Constitution. Now Citizenship Day ceremonies also include the reception of naturalized American citizens.

Rosh Hashanah—the Jewish New Year's Day—usually comes during September though it may also fall in the first week of October. The fall equinox occurs this month; Michaelmas, the Feast of St. Michael and all angels, is observed by members of the Greek and Roman Catholic Churches on September 29. There is an old proverb: "If you eat goose on Michaelmas Day, you will never want money all the year around."

In some localities, late in September, homage is paid to the Indians, America's "first citizens." Another September date—sponsored by the Kiwanis International—is Kids' Day, celebrated on the fourth Saturday to further the interests of our young people.

September is an especially important month in our calendar, and in several ways it is really more "a month of beginnings" than January is. The summer vacation is over; our public schools and colleges reopen; and countless clubs and varied organizations all

over the United States begin their programs and projects for another year.

September Birthstone—Sapphire

> Now glowed the firmament
> With living sapphires.
> —JOHN MILTON

The September birthstone—the sapphire, a variety of corundum
which is the hardest mineral except the diamond—is "a bright blue
precious stone that is hard and clear like a diamond." In ancient
times the true sapphire was called "hyacinthus."

Authorities disagree as to the origin of the word "sapphire"; some
sources say it comes from Latin and Greek, meaning "blue";
another believes that it is derived from a Sanskrit word, signifying
"beloved of Saturn."

The value of the sapphire depends upon its color. A strong, clear,
transparent and translucent "cornflower" blue is the most expensive.
One source says the hue may range from "inky blue through sky-
blue, to a pale grayish-blue." However, it is asserted that the color
should be "deep enough to show the richness of tint by daylight,
but light enough to retain color by artificial light."

This distinctive blue sapphire is the rarest type, and has been
found mostly in Kashmir. Such a natural stone commands about
the same price, carat for carat, as a good diamond does. Gems of
lesser quality compare in price with the topaz and aquamarine. A 3-
carat sapphire of the desired velvety blue may sell for from $450 to
$1800 or more.

Because of the lovely shade of this blue sapphire, its name
connotes a highly favored color—heavenly blue. Poets have often
sung of "sapphire" skies; and Thomas Gray wrote:

> He passed the flaming bounds of place and time;
> The living throne, the sapphire blaze,
> Where angels tremble while they gaze . . .

Sapphires also are found in other shades besides blue; and such gems include specimens of colorless white, green, purple, pink, yellow, and almost black.

When Marco Polo was on his famous travels, he mentioned seeing sapphires. Once when several men were journeying from Afghanistan to Delhi, India, they came across some beautiful blue stones in a mountain gap. They gathered as many as they could, placed them on their mules, and at the end of their trip, exchanged them for salt. Finally, someone recognized that these blue stones were really sapphires and sold them for high prices.

The sapphire mines in Kashmir were near the village of Soomjam in the Zanskar Range, at an altitude of 14,950 feet. When the old mines—discovered in 1881—became exhausted in 1927, a new source of supply was opened nearby. Many fine specimens were mined in this region.

The "Oriental topaz"—a yellow sapphire—comes from Ceylon. Siam has also produced splendid sapphires; its "Hill of Precious Stones" is famous for these gems. Other lands where these stones have been discovered include Bohemia, China, the Belgian Congo, Madagascar, Colombia, Rhodesia, and Tanganyika. Limited numbers of sapphires have also come from Queensland, in Australia; and in the United States, from near Helena, Montana, and in North Carolina.

Sapphires have for many years been most popular for use in jewelry; nowadays, because of their resistance to wear (like the diamond) these stones have many uses in modern industry. Recently they have been utilized for pivot jewels for wire-drawing dies, and for tools used to cut the sound tracks in moving picture films.

Ancient Greeks dedicated the sapphire to Apollo. Because of its heavenly blue hue they believed that if a person wore a sapphire, he would be certain to obtain an earlier and more favorable answer from the oracle. This stone was also considered a charm against unchastity, and various evil powers. This belief, it is said, was the reason that Pope Innocent II had all the bishops wear rings set with sapphires. St. Jerome once declared that the wearer of such a stone would be safe from capture, and could make peace with his enemies.

In her jewel collection, Marie Antoinette had several noted sapphires; the Russian royal regalia included some choice stones; of these sapphires, one weighed 260 carats, and was of "cornflower" blue. The largest such gem ever recorded was viewed in 1827 by a British Mission to Burma; this one weighed 951 carats.

A heart-shaped sapphire, dating from 1575, belonged to Lord Darnley, husband of Mary, Queen of Scots. The clergy of Aix-la-Chapelle gave Napoleon two large ones once used by Emperor Charlemagne as talismans.

These gems have played quite a role in British history. There is a story that Lady Scrope threw a sapphire ring out of the window to the Duke of Monmouth to confirm the death of Elizabeth I. Sir Hans Sloane (1660–1753) owned a fine sapphire among his jewels. When the government acquired his collection, it led to the founding of the British Museum. This particular sapphire was a deep blue one, a native Indian rose-cut stone weighing 35.5 carats.

The Duke of Devonshire was the possessor of a finely cut sapphire, 102 carats in weight, with the image of Buddha carved on it. In the center of the Imperial British Crown is the noted St. Edward's sapphire. When Edward the Confessor came to the throne in 1042, he wore this stone, mounted in a ring; it was rose-cut sometime in the seventeenth century. Catherine the Great of Russia had a blue sapphire, the third largest in the world.

At the back of the British crown is a sapphire that had been used in the state crown of Charles II. When James II fled to France, in 1688, he gave the gem to his son, the "Old Pretender." Later, with other Stuart treasures, the stone was bequeathed to George III. When Queen Elizabeth was crowned, this sapphire occupied the central position in her diadem just under the famous ruby, the "Black Prince"; and for George V, the sapphire was moved to the back of the crown.

Some exceptional sapphires can be seen in the United States. The collection of gems in the American Museum of Natural History in New York is considered one of the finest in the world. It includes the J. P. Morgan Collection, donated to the museum in 1905 by the financier. At that time it was valued at $200,000; today is no doubt worth much more.

In the Morgan Collection are two large sapphires: the "Star of India" (163 carats), the largest blue sapphire ever found, listed at $50,000, and the distinctive "Midnight Star" (116 carats), valued at $35,000.

In October, 1963, burglars succeeded in getting away with twenty-four jewels from the magnificent Morgan Collection, including the Star of India, the Midnight Star, the renowned "De Long" ruby, worth $21,400, a $10,000 engraved emerald, and other distinctive gems. Many of these are pictured in the Encyclopaedia Britannica section on jewels, so they are well-known and could not be sold intact without detection.

Early in January 1964, the District Attorney of New York, Frank Hogan, announced to the press that the famed Star of India sapphire and eight other of the stolen gems had been recovered. One of the three men accused of the theft accompanied officers to Miami, Florida, to try to locate the "mysterious keeper" of the jewels. One night about midnight, they received a communication that the gems were in a locker at a bus station in the downtown section of Miami. When a detective reached the depot at about 3 A.M., he found a water-logged leather bag, containing the noted jewels.

The party flew back to New York "after two days of hide and seek in the resort city that rivaled the plot of a detective novel." Dr. Bryan Mason of the Museum of Natural History identified the gems; however there was no certainty that the rest of the stones would be recovered.

It was found that the three suspects had been living in an expensive suite, at a New York hotel, and had been making frequent visits to the Museum just before the theft occurred. Police believe these men scaled the wall, gaining access to the J. P. Morgan Hall of Gems and Minerals, and carried off the gems from the glass cases. Now, luckily, the famous Star of India, is again in the museum for the public to admire.

September Flower—Aster

> And everywhere the purple asters nod
> And bend and wave and flit.
> —HELEN HUNT JACKSON

The September flower is the aster meaning "star." This is the common name for annuals and perennials of "several closely related genera of the aster or thistle family." This genus has about 250 species, found mostly in North America, but also in Europe, Asia, and South America.

There are—so it is claimed—about 175 in the Northeastern part of the United States and adjacent Canada. Others grow in the Rocky Mountain region, and also in California. Asters bloom from July to November; and when fall comes, the country east of Manitoba and Kansas and north of Tennessee is made beautiful by the lovely colors they add to the landscape.

> And asters by the brookside,
> Make asters in the brook.
> —HELEN HUNT JACKSON

The original asters had single blossoms and were unlike the large double flowers of today. It is reported that they were introduced into England in 1596 from Italy; and as early as 1637 several species native to America were taken to Europe from Virginia; others were imported from Amsterdam. By 1895 an American grower was listing 250 varieties.

Countless new ones have been developed by horticulturists, and these are quite different from the "parent forms." Thus "hybridization has resulted in a wide variety of color and habit." Now many of these hardy parennials are grown in gardens where they make decorative borders.

Asters differ much in height, growing from 6 inches to 6 feet in some cases. They have thin, erect stems; the leaves are alternate; and the foliage is fuller at the base of the plant than around the flowers themselves. Some blooms have double rays and look almost like chrysanthemums. The ray and disk are of different colors. The hues of the rays vary greatly; they may be white, purple, lavender, violet, red, rose, pink, cornflower, or sky blue. The disks usually are yellow, but often turn darker with age, becoming brown, red, or purple.

One of the most common, important, and best known is the "New England aster," which is the most showy of all. It is found from Massachusetts to Alberta, Canada, and then south to Alabama and New Mexico. This resplendent blossom grows 3 to 5 feet tall, and has large violet or purple rays; sometimes it measures 2 inches in diameter. The New England aster blooms in fields and swamps from August through September and into October, often after the first frost, and enhances the beauty of fall.

A very highly regarded plant of this genus is the "China aster," a summer annual. It has numerous varieties and more are being developed all the time, with marked diversity in form and color. In 1731, a Jesuit missionary brought back seeds of the China aster, which were planted in the Jardin des Plantes in Paris. He certainly did not foresee how much attention these flowers would get from growers in the next two centuries.

The China aster is a small, hardy plant with just one flower which has a yellow disk and lavender rays. It is a native of Eastern Asia, and has been cultivated for many centuries. The modern ones grow from 1 to 3 feet high. They are especially good as cut flowers, for they often last over a week.

Another aster with numerous varieties and "rich, warm, harmonious colors" is the "Michaelmas daisy," so named because it blooms around Michaelmas Day, September 29. This flower is considered the finest of the cultivated asters, and "par excellence the September flower."

It was developed by hybridizing three asters: the "New England," "New York," and "Italian." To grow well, the Michaelmas daisy needs rich soil, sunlight, and not too much summer heat. In England, the only native type of aster grows in salt marshes near the sea; but it is said that the Michaelmas variety—the cultivated species—really thrives better in the British Isles than in the United States. Often when the weather is mild in England these flowers bloom until Christmas.

> And, like proud lovers bent,
> In regal courtesy, as kings might woo,
> Tall goldenrods, bareheaded in the dew
> Above the asters bent.
> —HELEN HUNT JACKSON

Asters, besides giving beauty to our world, formerly were used in varied ways; these flowers were held sacred to the gods, and wreaths made from them were placed on altars at the temples. In medieval Europe it is said that the leaves of asters were burned to frighten away serpents; also the roots were crushed and fed to sickly bees; and at one period an ointment was concocted from asters and given to persons who had been bitten by mad dogs.

Alternate September Flower—Morning Glory

The alternate September flower, the morning glory, belongs to a family of woody or herbaceous vines, tropical shrubs and trees. The Greeks called it *Iponoea*, meaning "like bindweed." This was due to its ability to twine its stems tightly around a support, such as a wall, fence, window, or porch. The wild type was called "bindweed" in England, while the French termed the morning glory "Belle of the Day."

This plant is a quick growing one, cultivated for its showy flowers; and since it grows often to a height of 6 to 15 feet, it makes an excellent temporary shade or screen, and is often used for covering unsightly spots. The roots penetrate deeply, sometimes as much as 7 feet, and for this reason some call the plant the "Devil's Guts." It is "something of a rascal, when given too free a hand in the garden"; many farmers consider the morning glory a pest when its sturdy vines choke the young grain.

The plants produce blossoms from July to September, of such colors as blue, pink, white, purple, or lavender. The bright, fragile, funnel-shaped blooms sometimes are 3 to 5 inches in diameter. The delicate flowers open "at the first kiss of the sun," thus earning the name, "morning glory," and close as the day becomes brighter. One writer declared that nothing is more attractive than the "poise of those airy bells." This blossom attracts the bees. With its "five stiff little tracks," the insects can get to the supply of nectar without harming the delicate blooms.

Originating in tropical America, the ordinary morning glory now grows wild throughout North America, from Canada to Chile. This flower is a great favorite for its simple beauty, and for its self-sufficiency. After the first planting, it continues to grow and climb, but does not spread.

The first bloom of this kind was smaller, as described in 1621 by John Goodyear. Early growers in the British Isles received some seeds from Portugal and Spain. Sixteenth century Flemish and Dutch artists produced outstanding paintings of flowers and fruits. The cool blue and white morning glories were in striking contrast to the warm colors of other blossoms in their pictures.

Besides their usage in gardens, and as models for paintings, morning glories have been utilized in medicine. In France, for instance, they were boiled and mashed, and applied as a poultice to reduce swelling of the face.

A strange use for these flowers was discussed in July, 1964, when a Los Angeles physician, Dr. Sidney Cohen, reported in the *American Journal of Psychiatry* that two species of morning glories have been known to cause prolonged hallucinations, and in at least one case, led to suicide by a young university student.

After the victim had chewed three hundred seeds of the "Heavenly Blue" variety, he experienced hallucinations, which continued for twenty-four hours; and three weeks later, the attacks recurred. He feared he was losing his sanity; and not long afterwards, the young man met death while driving his car downhill at a high speed.

The Mexican variety—Heavenly Blue—was introduced in America in the 1830's. It is known that the Indians in Mexico had used the seeds to produce hallucinations. Some American "thrill-seekers" discovered this and also experimented with the seeds for such effects.

Another type of morning glory—"Pearly Gates"—was developed in the United States during the 1940's, and was found capable of causing attacks. A spokesman for the Food and Drug Administration stated that from 250 to 300 seeds must be consumed to bring about the illness.

Several distinctive varieties of the plant have been produced in Brazil and Japan. The Japanese people are devoted to morning glories, and have developed some with truly gorgeous colorings, and with a width of 7 inches. Originally in Japan, these flowers were grown only in temple gardens, and at that period, their blossoms were small. Then gardeners, outside the temple grounds, began to grow them, increasing both the size and number of shades.

There was a craze about morning glories in 1830, and a second one in 1896 (similar to the tulip fad in Holland). This resulted in rivalry between the various growers which created many new kinds, some of which were given quite poetical names.

Even though the morning glory has long been a favorite garden vine, it became much more popular when the distinctive Heavenly Blue from Mexico was introduced. Older artists usually painted the Virgin Mary wearing a blue robe. So the Mexicans called this particular flower the Virgin's Mantle.

The well known writer, Helen Hunt Jackson, has paid tribute to this humble but attractive flower in these lines:

> Wondrous interlacement!
> Holding fast to threads by green and silky rings.
> With the dawn it spreads its white and purple wings,
> Generous in its bloom, and sheltering while it clings,
> Sturdy morning glory.

October

There's something in October
Sets the gypsy blood astir . . .
—BLISS CARMAN

THE name of October, our tenth month, comes from the Latin
term *octo*, meaning "eighth." This was appropriate until the Romans changed their calendar to make it the tenth month. However, many realized the name was not correct; four times they tried unsuccessfully to change it. They made efforts to honor these four persons: Germanicus, an outstanding general; Antonius, an Emperor; Faustina, wife of Antonius; and Herculeus, the Emperor Commodus, who dubbed himself the Roman Hercules. But the old name, October, apparently suited the Romans better and they preferred to keep it.

In the Julian calendar October had thirty days; later, another was added. The Greeks and Romans both had several notable festivals in this month; one honored Mars, the god of war, and at that event the "October horse" was sacrificed to him. Another celebration noted the end of their military operations for the year.

In Northern European countries, October was known as "Wynmoneth" (wine month); for at this time the grapes were gathered and the wine was made. On their calendars they pictured this phase of the harvest season:

> Then for "October Month" they put
> A rude illuminated cut—
> Reaching ripe grapes from off the vine,
> Or pressing them or tunning wine;
> Or something to denote that there
> Was vintage at this time of year.

Early Germans called October "Winter-fyllith," or "fullith" because the winter season was supposed to begin at the time of full moon during this tenth month. On ancient calendars, the sport of hawking was often noted; also October was at times represented as a farmer, carrying a sack or sowing grain as was the custom this month. Edmund Spenser wrote:

> Then came October, full of merry glee. . . .
> Upon a dreadful scorpion did he ride.
> . . . and eeke by his side
> He had his ploughing share and coulter ready tyde.

Leigh Hunt told of corn planting and the setting out of fruit trees during October:

The chief business of October, in the great economy of nature, is dissemination, which is performed among other means by the high winds which now return.

With the coming of the autumn season there have always been those who get a feeling of melancholy as they watch life decay, and the frost kill the beautiful flowers; yet the month of October frequently is known for its fine weather. The middle of the day is usually warm and sunshiny and the air exhilarating.

One poet, Inez Rice, has written:

> October skips along the lanes,
> It kicks the leaves, and laughs with rains.

Sometimes there are rains and even snow flurries early in October; and such weather is termed "Squaw Winter," and is likely to be followed by "Indian Summer." In 1812 a New England writer declared:

Indian Summer is a charming season, which derived its name from the natives. They believe that it is caused by a wind that blows directly from the court of their great and benevolent god, Cautontowit.

These natives delighted in the warm spell; for during it they could hunt and lay in more food for winter. Also the women could gather nuts and their crops of maize. The pioneers, too, used this time to harvest the last of their pumpkins and root crops. The term Indian Summer spread even to England itself.

Lyn Harrington has given a fine word picture of this period:

Nature is soothing us before the cold and darkness of winter sets in. She is tucking in her family. The shrill tones of insects are almost silenced. Only a few late birds flash across the autumn sky. Most of the leaves have fallen to the ground, but next year's leaves are ready, tightly wrapped in their budcases.

One of the finest tributes ever paid this month was given by the American writer of prose and poetry, Helen Hunt Jackson. It is entitled *October's Bright Blue Weather* and begins with a comparison of this autumn month with June:

> O suns and skies and clouds of June,
> And flowers of June together,
> Ye cannot rival for one hour
> October's bright blue weather.

Then Mrs. Jackson continues by speaking of things that characterize this time: the yellow goldenrod, gentians, woodbine, colorful leaves, lanes "fragrant with grapes," ripening nuts, red apples "shining like jewels," and "lovely wayside things" sowing their seeds through the air. Then, the poet declares, "comrades seek sweet country haunts and like misers count the few remaining days of this delightful season," to which she pays this final tribute:

> O suns and skies and flowers of June,
> Count all your boasts together,
> Love loveth best of all the year
> October's bright blue weather.

October has always been associated with the turning and the falling of the leaves. The Slavs called it the "Yellow Month" because of the change in foliage. An unknown poet, in writing of the season said:

> Now Pomona pours her treasures,
> Leaves autumnal strew the ground . . .

And Edgar Allan Poe in rather sombre fashion tells us:

> The skies they were ashen and sober;
> The leaves they were crisped and sere,
> The leaves they were withering and sere;
> It was night in the lonesome October,
> Of my most immemorial year . . .

The more recent poet, Sara Teasdale, who has written unforgettable lyrics, penned these lines:

> The leaves fall patiently
> Nothing remembers or grieves;
> The river takes to the sea
> The yellow drift of leaves.

The fall in New England has been praised by countless persons; and Odell Shepherd, in his *October in New England* says in *God's World*, from COLLECTED POEMS (Harper & Row, 1956):

> And I not there to see . . .
> The flame of the maple tree.

And when that sensitive poet, Edna St. Vincent Millay, looked upon autumn beauty, she paid it an outstanding tribute:

> . . . Lord, I do fear
> Thou'st made the world too beautiful this year;
> My soul is all but out of me—let fall
> No burning leaf; prithee let no bird call.

October is one of two (November is the other) months that has given five Chief Executives to the White House: John Adams,

Rutherford B. Hayes, Chester Arthur, Theodore Roosevelt, and Dwight D. Eisenhower.

Others of distinction born in October are Richard III, Gandhi, Jenny Lind, G. W. Westinghouse, James Whitcomb Riley, Cervantes, Benjamin West, Watteau, Eleanor Roosevelt, Madame Helena Modjeska, William Penn, Noah Webster, and Eugene O'Neill.

Still others include Helen Hunt Jackson, Leigh Hunt, Sir Christopher Wren, Sarah Bernhart, Erasmus, John Keats, Johann Strauss, Captain James Cook, James Boswell, Franz Liszt, and Helen Hayes.

Many unusual and important happenings have taken place during October, such as: in 1066 the Battle of Hastings was fought; in 1535 the first complete English Bible was published; Mary, Queen of Scots was tried in 1586; in 1618 Sir Walter Raleigh was executed; in 1636 Harvard College was founded; in 1781 Cornwallis surrendered to Washington at Yorktown, Virginia; in 1789 President Washington issued the first Presidential Thanksgiving proclamation; and in 1791 the cornerstone for the White House was laid.

In 1793 Marie Antoinette was executed; in 1805 the Battle of Trafalgar and the death of Lord Nelson took place; in 1820 Spain ceded Florida to the United States; in 1836 Sam Houston became the first president of Texas; in 1846 there was the first public demonstration of the use of ether; in 1849 Edgar Allan Poe died; in 1854 the famous "Charge of the Light Brigade" occurred; and in 1859 John Brown made his noted raid on the U.S. Arsenal at Harpers Ferry, Virginia.

In 1861 the transcontinental telegraph line was completed; in 1867 the U.S.A. bought Alaska for about two cents an acre; in 1871 the great Chicago fire destroyed much of that city; 1879 saw the first incandescent light; in 1883 the Metropolitan Opera House opened in New York City; in 1884 Greenwich time was adopted; in 1889 the first Pan-American Conference was held; in 1890 the Mormon Church forbade polygamy; in 1904 the New York City subway trains started operating; in 1956 Queen Elizabeth II opened the world's first full atomic power plant; in 1957 Sputnick I was the first man-made satellite to encircle the earth; and in 1962 Walter M. Schirra made his orbital flight.

Besides being noted for its lovely fall colors, October contains some special days that are widely observed by varying groups. Many Americans take note of October 12, the anniversary of that important date, back in 1492, when the daring explorer, Christopher Columbus, reached the New World.

Poetry Day, October 15, calls our attention to the importance of this phase of literature and honors our poets. United Nations Day is celebrated on October 24; on the 27th (the birthday of Theodore Roosevelt), Navy Day is noted; and on the last day of the month young and old join in the celebration of Halloween.

Protestants observe Reformation Day on the fourth Sunday; our Canadian neighbors have their annual Thanksgiving on the second Monday in October; while two important Jewish holidays—Yom Kippur (Day of Atonement) and Sukkoth (Feast of Tabernacles) frequently fall in October.

October Birthstone—Opal

The opal, the gem dedicated to the month of October, has even from ancient days excited much admiration. Of it Pliny wrote these words:

Of all the precious stones, it is the opal that presents the greatest difficulty of description, it displaying at once the piercing hue of carbunculus, the purple brilliancy of amethystos, and the sea green of smaragdus, the whole blended together and refulgent with a brightness that is incredible.

The "precious opal" was highly rated; and the Romans classed it second only to the emerald. Its name is probably derived from the Sanskrit term, *upala*, meaning "precious stone." From this it may be assumed that the gem was first introduced to Europeans from India.

The stone is definitely different from all others; and it is impossible to create a synthetic one. The color changes in an opal are the most striking thing seen in modern jewelry. Here is how one source eulogizes the gem:

A rich internal play of colors in reds, blues, and greens gives rise to "precious opal," a beautiful and valuable gem stone.

These hues, it is said, are not in the opal itself, and can be seen only in a white light. The optical effect is due to "the breaking up of white light by interference"; also the colors change as the gem is viewed from different directions. Opals with a predominance of red flashes are the most sought after, although those with orange and green are also popular. The price of an opal depends on "the uniformity and brilliance of the color effects."

Owing to its unusual structure, an opal is susceptible to sudden changes of temperature, which may cause it to shatter, if, for instance, it is worn in arid regions. Light may have the same effect upon opals, some of which have cracked immediately after being taken from the ground. Heat can change the colors; and, as the gem is porous, it should never be immersed in any liquid. The strange things that can happen to an opal may account for the superstitions that became attached to the stone.

During the Middle Ages it was considered lucky to wear an opal; then thoughts of unpleasantries were gradually associated with it and it was considered unlucky to wear such a stone—unless the wearer was born in October. One opal, said to have been connected with much misfortune including several deaths, belonged to Alphonso XII of Spain. On his wedding day he gave his queen an opal ring; soon afterwards, she, the king's sister, and his sister-in-law, all died. Then, King Alphonso made the mistake of wearing the fatal ring and met with the same fate. After this the opal was placed around the neck of the Virgin of Almudena in Madrid.

One source says that owing to this "foolish" superstition in regard to the opal, the beautiful stone for many years "lay under a cloud." However, after black opals were discovered in Australia, the gem gained popularity, and now is worn extensively.

The oldest known opal mines were located in what was then Hungary, and is now Czechoslovakia. It is said that the Romans got their opals from this location. These mines are no longer worked to any extent as they produce only small stones. The Hungarian gems were sometimes called "Oriental opals," as they were taken to the Orient, and then shipped back to Europe.

Today the main source of supply for opals is Australia. The ones found there are larger than the Hungarian variety and show broader flashes of color. These first became known in 1877. In 1889 a hunter, tracking a wounded kangaroo, picked up an attractive stone in the White Cliffs district of New South Wales. If it had not been for this accidental discovery, the field might have lain undiscovered for years.

In 1905 a better source was discovered on each side of the boundary line of Queensland and New South Wales, where both black and white opals were deposited. The former, highly prized and quite rare, can be either black or gray, and are characterized by "scintillating blazes of red, orange, blue, green, purple."

In this Australian field, the stones are found in sandstone, rich in iron. The Coober Pedy field, in South Australia, is noted for its white opals, while fire opals have been discovered in West Australia. In the Stuart Range of South Australia, the gems have been found in light shades. Since 1890 rough opals, more than half of which go to England, have been mined; and they have been valued at more than a million and a half pounds (over $4,000,000).

There's an interesting story about the town of Coober Pedy. Its name is an aboriginal one and means "White Man in a Hole." The place got its start when opals were discovered there by some men in a camel train. At once hunters of these jewels trekked in from all over.

However, the heat was intense and there were no trees for shade. The men took a lesson from the wombat, a bear-like marsupial that burrows in the ground, and dug out homes for themselves. Today most of the buildings in Coober Pedy, including the post office, are underground.

Sid Latham has written about another Australian town, Anda-mooka, in the southwestern "Outback" of Australia. Here "the largest known opal"—the 203-carat "Andamooka" was found, along with millions of dollars worth of smaller opals.

Andamooka, according to Mr. Latham, "a damp hell underground and dusty oven above," is the locale of one of the largest opal lodes on the globe. But he declares, "There's no more hellish prospecting than the quest for fiery opals."

The Aussie diggers who engage in opal hunting here must endure heat up to 120 degrees in the daytime, while the thermometer at night often drops to 30 degrees. In addition, there are winds filled with red dust; and due to the scarcity of water, each man is allowed only twelve gallons per year.

The opals at Andamooka are found in a vein, varying in width from one inch to two feet. The men burrow along on their backs through tunnels. If a miner finds a rock he thinks may contain an opal, (if his saliva makes it show any gleam of color), he takes it carefully to the surface.

The opal is very fragile; its brittleness is the secret of its beauty. It can be squared off or rounded; but facets can not be cut in it.

When a digger finds a piece of opaline rock, he can usually sell it as soon as he makes his way out of the tunnel. Mr. Latham reported that one man, in ten minutes, sold an opal for which a company paid him $6,720.

Then the gems are cut and polished so all their scintillating colors are revealed. White opals are the most common, and black, the rarest and most highly prized. Mr. Latham said, too, that often the finest opals brought larger sums than diamonds of the same weight.

In Japan, white opals have been found, as have several varieties in India; other places from which opals come are Honduras, New Zealand, and the western part of the United States. In 1919 a fine black opal, weighing 17 ounces, was discovered in Nevada. This valuable gem was sent to the National Museum.

For some time Mexico has been noted for her fire opals from Hildalgo; now the supply there is apparently exhausted. These are quite transparent or translucent, with red and orange colors. A beautiful variety, the water opal, also has been found in Mexico.

In addition to their use as gems in jewelry pieces, today various forms of "common" opals are utilized in industry; certain ones are ground for abrasives; others serve as media for insulation; while some form part of the ingredients in ceramics.

It is said that the opal was the favorite stone of Queen Victoria. The "Devonshire" opal, from Lightning Ridge, New South Wales, is "a magnificent black opal, with splendid spangled coloration." It weighs about 100 carats, and is the property of the Duke of Devonshire. One of the finest opals of all times, called "Burning Troy," because of the many flashes it displays, was once worn by Josephine, wife of Napoleon. Perhaps the largest opal ever found, but one full of flaws, can be seen in the Imperial Cabinet in Vienna.

When Queen Elizabeth visited Australia in 1954, the government of South Australia presented her with a necklace containing an outstanding opal of 203 carats which had come from the Andamooka Field.

Alternate October Birthstone—Tourmaline

A person born in October has a choice of another semi-precious stone—the tourmaline. This is a complex mineral of varied composition, with "a glorious galaxy of colors." The single crystals are rarely uniform in hue, but contain several shades. When this stone is transparent and properly cut, it is a gem of great beauty. Light green tourmalines, when first taken to Europe, in the seventeenth century, were confused with emeralds, and sold as "Brazilian emeralds."

Tourmaline got its name from a Sinhalese word, *turmali*, that was applied to the small stones found in gravels in Ceylon. From there they were taken to Amsterdam in 1703. This stone has a strange quality; for it is "pyro-electric." If heat is applied to it or if it is rubbed (rubbing generates heat), the stone can attract pieces of paper. It is told that Dutch sailors used this stone for cleaning the ashes from their pipes.

Tourmalines are not very hard and therefore are not recommended too highly for ring settings, except for center stones (although they were often worn by Roman Catholic bishops in South America in signet rings.) Like some other gems, the lower grades are useful in industry; and today they are utilized in "tourmaline tongs, in measuring the intensity of radium emanations, and in optical work."

These stones come in a great variety of colors, but the rare light green is the most desirable. Authorities declare that tourmalines may be found "in almost any imaginable tint except the green of the emerald and the blue of the sapphire." Some are parti-colored; others are colorless, yellow, yellowish or brownish black, yellowish-green, or violet-red. The red variety, the rubellite (also found in pink) is quite attractive, but this kind is rarely found without flaws. Deep red tourmalines are said to be difficult to distinguish from Oriental rubies.

These gems are widely distributed throughout the world: Ceylon, Madagascar, Minas Gerais (in Brazil), Saxony, Switzerland, Upper Burma, Southwest Africa, Siam, Kashmir, and India. A black variety has been discovered in Cornwall, England; and especially fine crystals in pink, blue, and green come from both sides of the Urals, in Russia and Siberia. The Island of Elba has been noted for light-colored pink, yellow, and green tourmalines.

The stones were first found in San Diego County, in California, in 1872, when specimens of several hues, including red were discovered. The "Pale Chief Mine" produced excellent examples in large sizes. Some tourmalines have also come from the states of Maine and Connecticut.

October Flower—Calendula

> Look! the constant marigold
> Springs again from hidden roots.
> —ROBERT GRAVES

Calendula—the October flower—is the same as the marigold and received its Latin name because it was supposed to bloom on the

Kalends, the early part of each month. Calendula means "little-first-day-of-the-month"; and this plant "is willing to bloom the calendar through"—outdoors until a heavy freeze, and as a greenhouse flower the rest of the year.

In his book, *In the Gardener's Labyrinth,* Thomas Hall wrote this explanation:

The marigold, named of the herbaceous Calendula, is so properly termed, for that in every Calends, and in each month, this renewth of its own accord, and is found to bear flowers as well in winter, as in summer, for which cause, the Italians name the same "the flower of every month."

The calendula has been called marigold for many centuries, but it is also known by several other names. Because its bright face indicated cheer, and because it was dedicated to the sun, it was termed the "Bride of the Sun," "Gold Flower," and "Shining Herb." Other names included "Cowbloom" and "Yolk of Egg."

It is related that monks gave to the "Gold Flower" the prefix, "Mary," because all bright and beautiful things were supposed to belong to the Virgin Mary. The flower was dedicated to her, and in England was called "Mary's Gold," then slurred to "Marigold." Mary is said to have loved this blossom and often wore it in her bosom.

In primitive ages, the Greeks adorned themselves with garlands of marigolds at their wedding feasts. There also was a touching Greek legend about the origin of this flower. A maid named Caltha fell in love with the sun god; and each day she lived only to see him reappear. Caltha finally was consumed by her great passion, wasted slowly, and became a spirit. Then, where she had stood each morning watching for him, the first calendula appeared, its form and color resembling the sun.

Different ideas about this plant arose; some regarded it as an emblem of affection, others of grief, jealousy, envy, and fawning. In France some persons believed that if a young girl touched the petals with her bare feet, she would understand what the birds were saying. And if anyone ever dreamed of the marigold, this "denoted prosperity, riches, success, and a happy marriage."

At the time of Chaucer, the calendula was the "Gold Flower." By the time Keats was writing his poetry, it had become the marigold, and this is how he addressed them:

> Open wide your round of starry folds,
> Ye ardent marygolds.

Shakespeare, too, was devoted to this flower; and in his play, *Cymbeline,* he called it "Mary-bud." Another time he wrote these lines:

> The marigold that goes to bed with the sun
> And with him rises, weeping.

In the "Rape of Lucrece" the Bard of Avon wrote:

> Her eyes, like marigolds, had sheathed their light,
> And canopied in darkness, sweetly lay,
> Till they might open to adorn the day.

This plant has had an unusually interesting and sometimes contradictory history. One authority says it actually is a native of Mexico, and that is has "traveled a roundabout way before reaching our gardens." The story goes that Cortez saw this flower, when he conquered Mexico in 1520; then he carried seeds to Spain, but no one there seemed to take much interest in it. However, it did spread along the shores of the Mediterranean; and many Southern Europeans became acquainted with it.

The marigold was taken to Africa by the Moors, and was grown abundantly along the Algerian coast. When Charles V sent an expedition to free Tunis from the Moors in 1535, a soldier found what he thought was an African plant; then the marigold was reintroduced to Europe; and this variety has since been called the "African marigold."

These flowers were cultivated in France, and then taken to England by Huguenot refugees. This variety was known as the "French marigold." Since it was grown in pots, to use as a seasoning,

it received the name, "pot marigold." At the court of Henry VIII
and Anne Boleyn, many persons wore bouquets of marigolds and
pansies.

The plant was grown in old-fashoned gardens in the herb or
seasoning bed, and was not permitted to be raised among ornamental
flowers because of its unpleasant odor. Early botanists said that
"most choose to admire its charms at a distance."

Often the florets were dried and used to add flavor to soups,
stews, or drinks, especially in possets. A marigold wine was made,
too; and a pudding and conserve were concocted from the fresh
flowers, which were sometimes pickled or candied.

The petals could be substituted for saffron. Marigolds were
utilized as a toothache remedy, to dye hair, and as a cure for
smallpox and measles. Sometimes the ointment was rubbed on to
relieve the pain from the stings of bees or wasps; and some persons
used these flowers in amulets and love philters.

The calendula or marigold is a hardy annual, and easy to grow. It
likes hot weather, and blooms in gardens from midsummer until
frost if kept picked, and the weather is not too dry. The flowers—at
first single, later double ones—are bright and cheerful looking, with
petals ranging in color from cream to a rich yellow or deep orange.
The plant grows to the height of a foot, with scentless foliage.

Marigolds, some authorities say, reached the New World early in
the seventeenth century, and by 1856 there were fourteen varieties.
During the Civil War, according to one report, great quantities of
this plant were used to treat wounds and injuries.

David Burpee for many years had done research in developing
marigolds; and in 1932 he introduced a new "carnation-flowered
one" with the name, "Guinea Gold." An American missionary,
Carter D. Holton, of Riverside, California, found an unscented
marigold in northwestern China, on the border of Tibet; and from
this came the "Crown of Gold." In 1939 Mr. Burpee produced a
"Red and Gold" hybrid, the only African-French marigold on the
market. He also succeeded in getting red into tall varieties. In his
efforts to widen the range of colors, Mr. Burpee offered $10,000

for the first seeds that would grow pure white marigolds, and some nearly pure white ones have been produced.

This famous grower has been campaigning to give credence to the North American continent as the place of actual origin of the calendula or marigold, and has named one of his new types the "American Marigold." Two more Burpee products of 1961 were the "Mary Ellen" (a bright yellow) and the "Hawaii," named in honor of the fiftieth state, and described as:

. . . a deep orange and has slightly scented flowers and odorless foliage.
. . . It's one of the finest marigolds ever created.

For 1966 David Burpee introduced his "Yellow Nugget," a really different marigold, and a very prolific one. This dwarf species is of mixed parentage—with an American marigold for one parent and a French one for the other. The hybrid is said to be a profuse bloomer—flowering continuously from early summer until the frost comes. Of this new flower, A. C. McLeod has said: "Since it blooms so early and lasts so long, it can truly be termed ever-blooming."

Alternate October Flower—Cosmos

The cosmos, alternate October flower, is one of a genus of tropical herbs, numbering about twenty species. It is a tall, graceful, late-flowering annual or perennial, of many different varieties and feathery foliage.

The word "cosmos" is derived from the Greek term, *kosmos*, denoting "world" or "order." The root idea is that of orderliness, and signifies "an ornament or beautiful thing." And after seeing the lovely graceful cosmos in bloom, one feels that this flower has indeed been rightly named.

It is native to tropical and semitropical America. Its American ancestors are said to have come from the warmer uplands of Mexico. There are three species that grow in the United States, and these plants become more popular each year. The early kinds grown here could not stand cold, for the cosmos "glories in the sun." Often frost killed the plants before their seeds had ripened. However, new ones have been developed that now make the cosmos a fall as well as a summer flower.

The fact that the cosmos flowers late, when many other plants have completed their work, makes it of more value to gardeners and flower lovers. For it truly comes into its own at the first frosts. This late, aster-like blossom, with its filmy leaves, not only is most attractive in garden beds or against walls but the cut flowers make beautiful bouquets for indoor decorations.

The most commonly cultivated type in the United States may grow to heights of from 7 to 10 feet, though some are not so tall. It has smooth stems, and its brightly rayed, showy flowers have yellow disks. The rays are in a variety of colors including white, pink, red, purple, shell, yellow, orange—in fact, almost any hue except blue. The early primitive kinds had flowers only about an inch across. But various breeders have worked with this desirable plant, and have in some cases shortened the stems and increased the size of the blooms, some of which grow singly, others in clusters.

One kind—the Cosmus diversifolus—is a perennial grown from a tuberous root. It grows only about 16 inches tall, and its flowers have purplish rays and red centers.

The cosmos grows wild and extravagantly and at its very best in the Union of South Africa. Outstanding displays, comparing favorably with the great fields of poppies and lupin in the state of California, may be seen on the route from Johannesburg via Natal National Park.

For miles the roads on both sides are lined with hedges of these gracefully waving vari-colored white, red, and pink cosmos—great fields of them stretching away in the distance. Truly one of the most inspiring never-to-be-forgotten sights to behold.

November

No sun—no morn! No morn! no noon . . .
No shade, no shine, no butterflies, no bees,
No fruits, no flowers, no leaves, no birds,
November!

—Thomas Hood

NOVEMBER, now our eleventh month, retained its name (from the Latin, *novem,* denoting "nine") when January and February were added to the calendar. The Romans did try to change it, but were as unsuccessful as they were in their attempts at changing the names of other months. The Senate also tried to honor Tiberius by naming the month for him, but the Emperor refused to allow this change (even though his birthday fell during November) and said, "What will you do, Conscript Fathers, if you have 13 Caesars?"

In the Julian calendar, November had thirty-one days; then one was taken away and added to August, leaving the month with thirty days. This was considered an important month as winter set in on November 11. Ancient Saxons called November "Wint-monat," or "wind-month," because of the heavy gales prevalent then. It was customary for seamen to give up sea-faring, and to lay up their fishing craft on the beaches until the next spring, for they dared not risk their lives by fishing during the furious wind storms.

November was also dubbed "Blot-monath" or "blood-month," probably because it was during this time that they sacrificed animals to their deities; they also slaughtered cattle and salted the meat for winter use. Here is how Edmund Spenser referred to this custom in his poetry:

> Next was November; he rose full gross and fat
> As fed with lard, and that might well seem;
> For he had been a-fatting hogs of late . . .

Leigh Hunt comments that in November the farmers had finished their fall work, had given the animals shelter, and laid their implements by until the coming of another spring would call them back to their labors. Hunt admitted that November did have some drawbacks, but also several pleasant aspects. In speaking of the gloominess often prevalent at this time, he remarked:

A love of nature is the refuge. He who grapples with March and has the smiling eyes upon him of June and August need have no fear of November.

For many decades numerous people have considered this month the gloomiest one in the entire calendar, "the month of blue devils and suicides," with dull skies and fog—especially in cities like London. Often heavy rains shake the last leaves from the trees, leaving them completely bare; and the whole scene is one "not conducive to buoyancy and cheerfulness of spirit." In one of William Hone's books, we read:

> Ah, the year is fleeing from us;
> Bleak the day, and drear the night.

Long ago in the British Isles, there was a belief that November had an evil influence on the minds of men because of its monotonous, dreary days. In 1749 one church official, Bishop Warburton, wrote a friend:

I am now got hither to spend the month of November, the dreadful month, when the little witches drown themselves, and the great ones sell themselves to the Devil.

Our eleventh month furnished us five Presidents: James K. Polk, Zachary Taylor, Franklin Pierce, James Garfield, and Warren G. Harding.

Other interesting November personalities include Daniel Boone, Marie Antoinette, William Cullen Bryant, Rodin, Will Rogers, Sousa, Paderewski, Martin Luther, Oliver Goldsmith, Father Serra, Dale Carnegie, Louisa M. Alcott, and Winston Churchill.

Add to those, Mark Twain, Robert L. Stevenson, Robert Fulton, Monet, Nehru, Voltaire, Mendelssohn, Hetty Green, George Eliot, Marie Curie, Prince Charles, and Billy Sunday.

Here are some November events: in 1577 Sir Francis Drake ended his round-the-globe voyage; in 1635 the original settlement was made in Connecticut; in 1681 people had the first sight of Halley's Comet; in 1731 Benjamin Franklin started the first circulating library; in 1765 the Stamp Act went into effect; in 1776 the first permanent theater was established in America; in 1783 the British soldiers left America, and the Revolutionary Army was disbanded.

In 1783 also our first post office was founded; in 1789 we had the first national Thanksgiving Day; in 1800 Congress met for the first time in Washington, D.C.; in 1823 "Home, Sweet Home" was heard for the first time; in 1832 the first street railway in our land went into operation; in 1842 Mary Todd and Abraham Lincoln were married; and in 1858 the New York Symphony gave its initial concert.

In 1860 Lincoln was elected President; in 1863 he gave his memorable Gettysburg Address; in 1869 the first college football game was played; in 1881 the American Federation of Labor was started; in 1899, the first U.S. patent for an automobile was granted; in 1918 World War I ended; in 1926 the National Broadcasting Company had its first network; in 1952 our country exploded its first hydrogen bomb.

In the churches of Western Christendom, November 1 and 2 are celebrated as All Saints Day and All Souls Day—perhaps replacing an old Celtic feast of the dead.

In the United States, general election day comes on the first Tuesday after the first Monday in November. On November 11, Veterans Day (formerly Armistice Day) is observed in honor of service men and women of all wars. And when the fourth Thursday arrives, Americans celebrate Thanksgiving Day—usually with family get-togethers. This day was first noted by the Pilgrims in Massachusetts to express their heart-felt gratitude for a bountiful harvest.

Nowadays November is no longer considered such a gloomy month; especially in the United States where there are exciting football contests, family dinners, and other festivities that serve as a prelude to the even gayer Christmas holiday season.

November Birthstone—Topaz

The topaz, birthstone for those born in November, is the most popular and highly valued yellow stone today. In early periods, all transparent yellow gems were termed "topaz"; but at the present time, the word is applied by dealers only to the yellow type of quartz, known as "citrine." This is characterized by its "warm glowing, golden shades from light yellow to dark gold." The true topaz is a fine rare stone and commands high prices.

Usually the topaz is water clear, colorless, or of yellowish hue. But because of the presence of different coloring matters, they may be of other colors—mainly light ones. There is a bluish-green topaz that resembles the aquamarine, while some brownish stones, when treated with heat, take on an attractive rose-pink shade.

This gem is fairly hard, exceeded only by the diamond and the corundum in this respect. A topaz takes on a dazzling polish, and when properly cut is a most distinctive jewel. The stone is easily cleaved, if the work is properly done. These gems are cut in brilliant and step forms and often set in red or yellow gold and surrounded by small diamonds.

There are different opinions as to the origin of the world "topaz."

Pliny declared it came from the name of an island in the Red Sea; but some discount this. Others believe it is derived from the Greek "Topazas" ("top" means to "shine") or from the Sanskrit word that signifies "heat" or "fire."

Although these stones have a world distribution, Siam was noted as their early home. Topazes have been discovered in such places as Rhodesia, Northern Nigeria, Madagascar, Japan, Upper Burma, Indo-China, Siberia, New South Wales, Tasmania, in the Mourne Mountains of Ireland, Norway, Sweden, Saxony, Cornwall in England, Scotland, and Czechoslovakia. In the United States the gems have been found in California, Colorado, Utah and New Hampshire.

Most of the topazes now used for setting in jewelry come from Brazil, in the state of Minas Gerais. The "Imperial" or "Precious" is rare in weights above 10 carats; and it is a brilliant gem in varying shades. One source states that "It is usual to refer to the true topaz, as a 'Brazilian topaz'."

One of the world's most famous and beautiful topazes is the 1,680-carat "Braganza" in the Portuguese Crown Jewels. At first, this was mistaken for a yellow diamond. In the British Museum in London there is a rough opaque crystal of topaz which was found in Norway, weighing 137 pounds. Brazil furnished this same institution one of 29 pounds. Another large specimen of this type, also from Brazil, can be viewed in the American Museum of Natural History in New York.

A story is told of a clear and colorless "pebble" of 13 pounds which was for many years used as a doorstop in a London tea shop on Fleet Street. It was considered just "a lump of glass" until an expert examined the "pebble" and discovered it had "the perfect cleavage of the topaz."

Cleopatra is said to have been especially fond of topazes for they reminded her of honey. Ancients called this gem "the stone of strength," and believed that it brought the warmth of friendship to its wearer; also that it had the power to prevent unpleasant dreams, and to dispel worry and trouble from human minds.

November Flower—Chrysanthemum

> Why should this flower delay so long
> To show the tremulous plumes . . .
> Too late its beauty, lonely thing,
> The season's shine is spent.
> Nothing remains for it but shivering
> In tempests turbulent.
> —THOMAS HARDY

Our November flower, the incomparable chrysanthemum, belongs to one of the largest families of plants—Compositae—and has developed countless varieties. It is found all around the globe; on the continents of Europe, Asia, Africa, and America; and is grown by amateurs and commercial nurseries.

A few bloom in August and September, but most of them flower in October. Even though the chrysanthemum is a fall blossom, it loves the sun; appears to try to produce as many seeds as possible before the arrival of frosts. Often, when practically all other flowers have died, the chrysanthemum still challenges the beauty of autumn trees, shrubs, and vines with "a lively show of colors."

This plant gets its name from two Greek terms, and means "Golden Flower." It is a sturdy, hardy plant, grows in clumps, has leafy stems, and sends out a pungent fragrance.

The flower heads vary greatly, but they always have many rays. There is "the immense showy hothouse flower" of giant size produced by the careful nurture of the professional. This type is often used as a corsage for one attending a football game, also for house and table decorations. It is truly representative of the skill of the horticulturist.

In decided contrast to this variety is the tiny pompom so popular at the present time. Chrysanthemums vary also in their coloring, which may range from "pale yellow to chestnut, or pink to crimson"; white ones, too, are popular. Because of their infinite variety these blooms are among the world's loveliest ones, both for outdoor growth and as cut flowers. One authority has stated:

The chrysanthemum has led such a mixed-up over-civilized life that to-day it is available in almost any color and a vast choice of shapes.

All the varied forms of this plant are said to have originated after 3,000 years of cultivation from an "unknown race of Chinese perennials," or, perhaps, from "a wild Siberian ancestor," as one source has termed it. In 500 B.C. Confucius praised this flower for its "yellow glory." It has been said that "long before the birth of Christ the chrysanthemum was regarded as the symbol of longevity and perfection."

The Chinese are said to have cultivated the chrysanthemum long before the Romans had developed their love for roses and carnations. It was considered sacred in China and used for temple adornment; woven into rugs; embroidered on fine brocades; and painted on delicate porcelain. The Chinese Empress herself is reported to have been present at the planting of chrysanthemums.

There is a story dating back many centuries, that once some Chinese travelers went to Japan for a visit, and took with them several of the plants. The Japanese were so delighted with the gift that they immediately began to cultivate the flower. During the fourteenth century the Mikado made the conventionalized form his emblem. So, while the flower is termed the national emblem of Japan, the honor really should go to China. In A.D. 900 the Mikado held a Chrysanthemum Show; and when the Japanese waged their "War of the Dynasty" or "The Chrysanthemum War" (which started in 1357), each warrior wore a yellow chrysanthemum as "a golden pledge of courage."

The Emperor's Order of the Chrysanthemum is Japan's highest honor. (One authority asserts that the emblem on the Japanese flag does not represent the rising sun—as is generally believed—but really stands for sixteen chrysanthemum petals.)

For many years these flowers could be grown in Japan only in the Mikado's gardens, or in those of the nobility. But nowadays all classes of Japanese, young and old, grow these artistic blossoms; and each fall many persons take part in the Chrysanthemum Festivals.

Both the Chinese and Japanese have also for centuries produced works of art that feature the distinctive blooms.

By the beginning of the seventeenth century, chrysanthemums had been introduced into Europe. One variety, called the "Paris Daisy," was grown in that city before 1629. An old Dutch garden book of 1690 listed 1,750 Chinese plants that had been received in Holland, and the "Golden Flower" was among them.

Its popularity grew and the plant reached the British Isles, it is said, in 1699. Some were grown in gardens in Chelsea in London, in 1734, then were lost, and not seen again until 1796. By 1790 a purple chrysanthemum had reached the noted Kew Gardens near London. Between 1820 and 1830, England imported about seventy kinds from China and Japan. One, named the "Chinese Drunken Lady," had a rosy hue. Many gardeners welcomed the new plants; and they were cultivated not only in aristocratic gardens, but in window boxes of humble cottages as well.

In 1832 chrysanthemum seeds were raised for the first time in England. Robert Fortune went to the East to introduce China tea to India, and while on the Island of Chusan, off the coast of China, he came across some new types of the flowers. In 1846 he brought two back to England which were the ancestors of the pompom variety, one, named the "Chusan Lady;" the other, a button-flowered type.

Some large chrysanthemums reached the British Isles about 1860, and soon it became the fashion to cultivate these gigantic types. In 1880 one plant sold for $1500. By the end of the nineteenth century the English gardeners were producing in greenhouses such large specimens that they "could not be put in a man's hat."

In the United States for many decades numerous kinds of the coveted plants have been raised; but it wasn't until 1944 that the National Chrysanthemum Society was founded, with the motto, "Cheerfulness under adversity, integrity, goodwill."

Among the growers who have specialized in this plant are Dr. and Mrs. Hugh D. Wilson of Los Angeles. They have carefully cross-bred plants and now have thirty varieties that are not only attractive but actually have scent. This couple began hybridizing in 1954; and the following year, they "happened onto 'Loretto,' their first scented mum, and the first with fragrance to be patented in the United States."

This particular flower, patented in 1958, has a jasmine odor. The Wilsons have also patents pending on three other scented varieties: "Mayor of Hollywood" (like sweet alyssum); "Golden Essence" (like magnolia); and "Rosette" (like old rose).

There's a place not far from Pasadena, California, where visitors can see countless varieties of modern chrysanthemums at their very best. This is the distinctive Sunnyslope Nursery where several acres are devoted exclusively to the raising of these autumn favorites.

The best time to see the gorgeous displays is late in October or early November. At the entrance is a dark red gateway, or torii, so characteristic of the landscape in Japan.

At once one is overwhelmed by the beauty and variety of the plants which grow in clumps, some under shelter, others in the open field. There are "mums" of every imaginable color, shape, and size. Large beautifully developed blooms contrast with the dainty ones of the pompom type.

And it's interesting to see the contrasting colors; at times those of a deep rose shade hobnob with others in hues of light pink; and rich rusty colored blooms form an excellent foil for yellow or dainty white flowers.

To see these gardens, with their incomparable flowers, the background of eucalyptus foliage, and Old Baldy rising in the distance, is a beautiful and unforgettable scene.

Today new mums are being developed by nurseries in an effort to evolve varieties that will bloom earlier. Some of them are in pastel shades, while others show brilliant, striking colors.

E. S. Boerner, plant research director for the Jackson and Perkins firm, has just introduced four new ones: "Golden Eagle," a bright gold yellow, over five inches across, which blooms early in September; "Brown Lark," a rich strawberry bronze that provides a wealth of warm color for the garden; "Tufted Duck," a clear lavender pink, six inches in diameter; and "Chewink," bright burgundy red, with exceptionally long stems (this kind blooms from late in September until severe frosts come).

Like some other plants, chrysanthemums have been used as food. The Chinese, for instance, served the petals in salads; the Italians, as an herb; and one type, "Feverfew," was utilized in medicine. Some persons believed the flower was a good remedy for opium users, and for vertigo. It is said that it also helped those who were "melanchol-like, sad, pensive, and without speech." Early in New England one kind was fashioned into small bouquets which church attendants smelled in order to keep awake during those long sermons. In Peru, and also in the Caucasus Mountains, chrysanthemums were culti-vated for use in an insecticide.

Several stories are connected with this important and outstanding plant. One tells of a stream whose banks were lined with the flowers. As the petals fell into the water, people drank it, for the belief was current that it would make them live much longer.

Another legend has it that when the Three Kings, or Wise Men, reached Bethlehem, they found no signs of rejoicing over the birth of the Christ Child. They made their way through the narrow streets, but were not able to find the manger. Suddenly King Melchior stopped the camels; for he saw a flower whose petals were rayed like the bright star that he and his companions, the other Magi, had followed to Bethlehem.

As the three men gazed at the blossom, and then looked upward at the bright star, the stable door opened of its own accord. King Melchior bent down, plucked the flower, and the three dismounted and went into the stable. There, at the manger, King Melchior placed the flower, a chrysanthemum, in the Baby's hand. As the Magi knelt in devotion, the Christ Child held the blossom that had guided them to Him like a scepter.

And now, many centuries later, we still admire this unusual flower that has had a long and interesting role in history. The Japanese call it "Kiku," and they believe:

. . . the orderly unfolding of its petals marks perfection. . . . Coming at the ripeness of the year, it symbolizes human perfection.

December

And after him came the chill December;
Yet he through merry feasting which he made,
And great bonfires, did not the cold remember
His Saviour's birth his mind so much did glad.

— EDMUND SPENSER

THE name of our last month of the year, December, means "tenth," from the Latin *decem*. Like the three preceding months, it has been misnamed ever since the Romans added two months to their year. One Emperor, Commodus, suggested that since his mistress had been painted as an Amazon, the name of December should be changed to "Amazonius" in her honor; but his request was not granted. Several times the Roman Senate attempted to change the name, but the old one remained on the calendar.

In the Julian Calendar December had thirty days; later one more was added, making it the present thirty-one. During this month, beginning December 17, the Romans celebrated one of their most important festivals, the Saturnalia, which was noted for its excesses. This feast was to honor the god of seed-sowing, Saturn, who was said to have reigned during the "Golden Age."

The twelfth month has been termed by different writers by such names as "Fumosus" (smoky), because of the great amount of smoke that poured from chimneys at this season; "Gelidus" (frosty); also "Canus" (hoary) because deep snow covered the ground in December.

Early Saxons named it the "Winter-monath" or "Midwinter" as it was halfway between autumn and spring. Their great feast, dedicated to Thor, ancient god of thunder, was observed at the time of the winter solstice, about December 21. This celebration was called "Giul," from a word, denoting "ale," later corrupted to "Yule." After the Saxons had accepted Christianity, they named December the "Heiligh-monath" (holy month) because of the birthday of Christ.

From early times, the month of December was considered an extremely cold period, to judge from the way poets described it. The first quotation is from the *Poetical Calendar:*

> Last of the months, severest of them all,
> Woe to the regions where thy terrors fall!
> For lo! the fiery horses of the sun
> Through the twelve signs their rapid course have run.
> Time like a serpent, bites his forked tail
> And Winter, on a goat, bestrides the gale.

In 1799 John Nathan Hutchins penned these lines:

> Now days are short, nights long and raw,
> With pinching frost, and slabby rain and snow;
> But let good rousing fires, and Christmas cheer,
> Still mix'd with charity, conclude the year . . .

William Shakespeare, too, wrote of winter days:

> When icicles hang by the wall
> And Dick, the shepherd, blows his nail,
> And Tom bears logs into the hall,
> And milk comes frozen in the pail,
> When blood is nipt, and ways be foul,
> Then nightly sings the staring owl . . .

Leigh Hunt, whose vivid descriptions of other months and seasons have been quoted, says of December conditions:

It is now complete winter . . . the farmer does little or nothing outdoors . . . and the trees look but skeletons of what they were. But

December has one circumstance in it that turns it into the merriest month of the year—Christmas.

The celebration of this most important feast day, from Christmas Day itself until Twelfth Night on January 5, was carried on by rich and poor alike, in great manor halls and in humble cottages. For it was the crowning time of all the year; and its joys have been sung over and over in many lands:

> Bring more wood, and set the glasses,
> Join, my friends, our Christmas cheer.
> Come, a catch, and kiss the lasses,
> Christmas comes but once a year.
> —WILLIAM HONE

And at a more modern date, Alfred Tennyson, when Christ's birthday was approaching, was impressed by the ringing of the Christmas church bells in distant villages:

> They bring me sorrow, touched with joy,
> The merry, merry bells of Yule.

Some English colonists to the New World happily carried their native holiday customs with them; and James Russell Lowell has thus described a Christmas scene:

> Within the halls are song and laughter;
> The cheeks of Christmas grow red and jolly;
> And sprouting is every corbel and rafter
> With lightsome green of ivy and holly,
> Through the deep gulf of the chimney wide
> Wallows the Yule-log's roaring tide . . .

Even though for centuries December has been regarded as a time of hard frosts and heavy snowstorms, in recent years conditions have changed in some localities, and milder weather has prevailed.

Three of our Chief Executives observed their natal dates in December: Martin Van Buren, Andrew Johnson, and Woodrow Wilson.

They shared this month with other prominent personages such as Mary, Queen of Scots, Thomas Carlyle, Horace, Eli Whitney, John

Milton, Beethoven, Jane Austen, John Greenleaf Whittier, Charles Wesley, Sir Isaac Newton, Louis Pasteur, James Thurber, Charles Goodyear, and William Gladstone.

Also born in the last month of the year were Rudyard Kipling, Lord Cornwallis, Andre Kostelanetz, Willa Cather, Clara Barton, James A. Doolittle, Rudolph Friml, Kit Carson, Margaret Mead, Walt Disney, and General James Oglethorpe.

Among the historical December events are these: in 1065 Westminster Abbey was dedicated; in 1776 General Washington crossed the Delaware River; in 1782 the Mason-Dixon Line was established; in 1784 American Methodism started in Baltimore, Maryland; in 1791 the Bill of Rights was adopted; in 1799 George Washington died; in 1803 the United States purchased the Louisiana Territory from France; and the first Bible Society was started in America in 1808.

Also in 1816 gas was used for the first time for lights; in 1823 came the enunciation of the Monroe Doctrine; 1843 saw publication of Charles Dickens's *A Christmas Carol;* in 1848 the first gold from California was deposited in the United States mint; in 1851 the first American Y.M.C.A. was begun in Boston; in 1859 John Brown was hanged; in 1869 the Knights of Labor, the first important labor union, was founded; in 1871 the first performance of Verdi's *Aida* was given in Cairo, Egypt to celebrate the opening of the Suez Canal; and in 1901 the first Nobel Prizes were awarded.

In 1903 the Wright Brothers flew at Kittyhawk, North Carolina; in 1907 the first Christmas seals went on sale; 1933 saw the end of Prohibition; in 1937 Edward VIII of England abdicated; in 1941 the United States declared war on Japan after the bombing of Pearl Harbor on December 7; in 1946 President Truman proclaimed the cessation of hostilites of World War II; and in 1958 there was the first successful Atlas firing.

Although Christmas is the most popular and most widely observed day in December, around the world, the final month of the year also has several other days that are worthy of note. For example, December 15, the day in 1791 the first ten amendments to the Constitution were ratified, is celebrated as Bill of Rights Day by Presidential proclamation. This holiday stresses the importance of these amendments to all individuals in America.

December 21 is noted—mostly in the New England states—as Forefathers' Day, to commemorate the landing of the Pilgrims at Plymouth on December 21, 1620. The day after Christmas, December 26, has for centuries been termed St. Stephen's Day, to honor the early martyr who was stoned to death. In an old carol, *Good King Wenceslaus* we learn that he ". . . looked out on the Feast of Stephen . . ." and then with his page he distributed food and fuel to a poor neighbor.

For some unknown reason St. Stephen was associated with horses; and certain customs connected with these animals were carried out on his feast day, December 26.

This same date is also known as Boxing Day and celebrated in the United Kingdom, Australia, some Canadian provinces, and in Poland, as a time for giving gifts, especially to servants, or others, such as postmen, porters, etc., who had served people throughout the past year. In some places it was customary for the ministers in churches to open the Mite Boxes and distribute their contents—food, clothing, or money—to needy parishioners.

The day after Christmas has also, for many years, been an important one in the British Isles; for on it came the opening performance of the holiday pantomime, so dear to the hearts of children who look forward to it each year. These fanciful concoctions have often had leading actors and actresses in top roles.

On December 28 some churches celebrate Childermas, or Holy Innocents' Day, in memory of those young children put to death in Bethlehem by order of King Herod.

In December the Jews observe their eight-day Chanukah (Hanukkah), or Feast of Lights, to recall the freeing of their temple in Jerusalem from the Syrian invaders. Nowadays the idea of this national victory has been "subordinated to a spiritual theme—the relighting of the temple and its rededication." This feast has also come to be "symbolic of steadfastness of faith against the oppressor and of the fight for religious freedom."

December Birthstone—Turquoise

The turquoise, December birthstone, an opaque, greenish-blue stone is a mineral which has been used as a gem, and for ornamental purposes for countless centuries. As early as 3400 B.C. the Egyptians were obtaining such stones from the Sinai Peninsula. Later very good ones were discovered in Persia and taken to France via Turkey.

The word "turquoise" (French for "Turkish") is also spelled "turkoise," "turquois," and "turkis." Some say the term is of Tartar origin, coming through Turkestan (or perhaps because the gems passed through Turkish hands).

The turquoise is one of the few opaque stones of value that is desired for its color alone. The shades may vary from the comparatively scarce "sky blue" (or "robin's egg blue") and pale blue to a greenish blue and pale sea green. This gem retains its color under artificial light; however, some authorities assert that all turquoises have a tendency to become green with age.

This last is said to be caused when water enters the porous stone; a chemical change affects the hue, turning it to a bluish or yellowish green. Therefore, when wearing a turquoise ring, the owner should remove it before washing her hands. This gem should never be immersed in any liquid. Other agents which can affect the color are grease, soap, and perspiration. Some turquoises have faded when first exposed to the light; and one source says that all will fade in the course of time.

Heat can alter the shade, too; and since this gem is rather soft, it does not retain a high polish. But in spite of such drawbacks, the stones have long been desirable for jewelry; in rings, they are set en cabochon. A turquoise of good shade set in contrasting gold and surrounded by small diamonds makes a very attractive ring.

The finest turquoises still come from Iran (Persia); and large blue stones are more highly valued in the East than elsewhere. Ancient turquoise mines at Nishapur were known to the Egyptians as early as 4,000 B.C. Although none of the gems were found in India, many passed through that country on their way to the European markets. A Major MacDonald rediscovered the early mines at Nishapur, and in 1857, exhibited some of the stones in Egypt. These Persian mines—so it is said—are still producing as fine specimens as they did ten centuries ago.

Other sources of supply are the Sinai Peninsula, Tibet, Turkestan, Abyssinia, Siberia, Australia, Mexico, and Central America. Pale blue to green turquoises are found in this country, in New Mexico, in San Bernardino County, California, Nevada, Utah, Texas, Arizona, Colorado, and Virginia.

Before Cortez conquered Mexico, American Indians were working the prehistoric mines in the Cerrillos District, located in the north central section of New Mexico. This locality is an important source of supply, as some of the old mines are still being worked at the present time.

It is said there are few gems that "link together present-day usage with the glamour and romance of the past as does the opaque sky blue turquoise." Orientals prized the gem very highly, as is evidenced by the carved and decorated objects of art that show their highly developed culture. In Egypt, Arabia, Turkey, and Persia, these stones were often engraved, also mounted in rings, sword sheaths, daggers, and saddles. And in faraway South America, in early times, the Incas used turquoises in their artistic mosaics.

Perhaps the finest turquoise ever mined—the property of the Shah of Persia—was an outstanding specimen, three and one-half inches long.

In 1900 some explorers opened the tomb of the Eygptian Queen Zer, who was buried more than 8,000 years ago. Among the choice treasures found with her were four bracelets, set with alternate plaques of cast gold and carved turquoises. They had been on the arm of the dead queen for many centuries, yet the stones were as clear and bright as when they had been placed in the tomb. These turquoise-set pieces of jewelry are no doubt among the oldest in existence.

Shakespeare referred to the high value of this gem, when in his drama, *The Merchant of Venice*, he had Shylock say he would not lose his turquoise for a wilderness of monkeys.

The stone was regarded as a talisman of love; it was certain to preserve the fidelity of friends, prevent bodily harm, and bring good luck and prosperity to its owner. According to an old belief, a turquoise should be *given*, not bought. And by changing its color, it was believed that a turquoise could betray a wife's infidelity. Here is an excerpt from an early writer, in regard to the power of this gem:

A turquoise given by a loving hand carries with it happiness, and good fortune. . . . The color of the turquoise pales when the well-being of the giver is in danger.

Alternate December Birthstone—Zircon

The alternate December birthstone, the zircon, a semi-precious one, "is essentially an Oriental stone," and has been seen much longer in shops in Burma and Ceylon, than in Europe or the United States. Sometimes it has been called the "Mystery stone," because of its mineral components.

The high reflective index and the high dispersion cause the zircon to approach the diamond in fire and brilliance. One admirer has commented, "The colorless stones rival even diamonds in splendour of brilliance and display of fire."

This stone has had several names, and the origin of the word, "zircon" is not certain. It may be derived from the Arabic, *zargun*, meaning "vermillion," or a Persian term, denoting "gold-colored."

Zircons are widely distributed around the world, and are found in igneous (fiery) rocks. The crystals appear as four-sided prisms, or as worn water pebbles. The stones have long been discovered and prized in Ceylon, which is still the chief source for those used in making jewelry. These gems also come from Burma, Thailand, Indo-China, the Urals of Russia and Siberia, Madagascar, South Africa, France, Norway, New South Wales, New Zealand, and around Ontario and Quebec in Canada. Zircons have been found along the east coast of Florida; in Essex and Orange Counties, New York; the Pike's Peak district of Colorado; and in Henderson County, North Carolina.

Although the zircon is not very hard, and therefore not too suitable for mounting in a ring, "nature has compensated by giving it a range of color." Its high refraction and exceptional shades also make it a valuable gem stone. Zircons may be colorless, yellow, yellowish-brown (from South Africa); red (from France or Australia); leaf green, blue, bluish-green, or orange.

Ceylon has produced many of the finest ones used in jewelry. Their best were at first thought to be diamonds. The colorless variety from this locality is called a "mature diamond." When the native yellow Ceylonese stones are subjected to heat (which removes the colors), the stones are "jargons." When these colorless, transparent gems, cut as brilliants, have a decided display of fire, especially in dim light, they make better imitations of diamonds than any other stone.

The most popular zircon today is the beautiful artificially produced sky blue variety that first appeared on the market in 1914.

A steel blue gem is of great brilliancy and dispersion when cut. The color is said to be obtained by heating the yellow Siamese stone.

However, it is claimed that some artificially produced blue gems turn brown when exposed to bright sunlight. There are pale blue zircons that resemble aquamarines, but they are cheaper than aquamarines or sapphires. One authority believes that some blue zircons *do* occur natural form, but that they may have been treated by nature herself. Small bluish crystals have been discovered in the lava of Mt. Vesuvius; and in some cases, on exposure to light, they make rapid and unusual changes in tint.

One collector, Sir Arthur Church, spent many years gathering zircons. His outstanding collection, "a marvelous series of zircons of various shades of colors," can be seen at the British Museum.

Experts assert that this attractive and semiprecious gem has not yet been fully appreciated; that most persons are not familiar with it; and that it should be used in more pieces of jewelry.

Not only are zircons utilized for ornamentation, but they are important in the field of industry; for they are used in the manufacture of steel and abrasives.

December Flower—Narcissus

The December flower—the narcissus—is a genus of bulbous plants of the Amaryllis family. Its name comes from the Greek term *narke,* denoting "narcotic, or capable of producing stupor," as Pliny stated centuries ago. The Greeks believed this plant gave off evil emanations. Tradition had it that this scent was harmful, could cause headaches, madness, and even death.

The narcissus is native to the warmer parts of the Old World—Central Europe; the Mediterranean region; and the East, including China and Japan. From early wild varieties many modern types have been produced; and now this is a most popular plant grown extensively in gardens round the world. It is well liked for its early blooming, its fragrance, and its beauty; the stalks have narrow grasslike leaves, and the blooms are of varied colors, usually white, yellow, or orange-yellow.

The British imported many bulbs from the Continent, where the Dutch produced fine varieties. The Turks were excellent gardeners, and also created new kinds. The narcissus has its place in heraldry, too, and appears on the coat of arms of a London borough—Lambeth—and on that of Cardiff, Wales.

There are said to be sixty-five kinds of narcissus under cultivation, divided into eleven groups by the Royal Horticultural Society. Among the better-known ones are "Pseudo Narcissus," the "Polyantheus," and the "Poet's Narcissus."

The Pseudo Narcissus is often found in wooded areas of many parts of Europe, and also grows in the United States. (The daffodil falls under the classification of the "pseudo.")

"Narcissus Tazetta" belongs to the Polyanthus, or bunch narcissus, as does the jonquil. "Tazetta" means "little cup," and this variety was found not only near the Mediterranean but also in Syria, Persia, Kashmir, China, and Japan, where it grew from time immemorial. In the East it was given such names as the "Sacred China Lily," "New Year's Lily," "Good Luck Flower," and because of its ability to grow in water, "Water Fairy Flower."

The Poet's Narcissus (or "Pheasant's Eye") was being cultivated in England before the sixteenth century. It is pure white with a shallow, wrinkled reddish crown. There are various hybrids of this variety, and its blossoms may be single, double, white, yellow, pink, cream-colored, orange or orange-red.

Some people believe the narcissus originated in Greece (although it has been found in funeral wreaths in Egypt, with mummies of the eighteenth dynasty). Several species are native to the Greek peninsula; and from primitive times narcissi have been woven into the myths, legends, and early religion of the Greeks. They represented the Eumenides or Furies as having the flowers twined in their harsh locks, and they were supposed to terrify their victims. In Greek tombs well preserved wreaths of these blossoms have been found; someone has said, "When the dead went to the underworld, they wore crowns of white narcissus that friends had placed there."

The blind bard Homer, in his *Hymn to Demeter*, described this flower as "glittering, a noble sight for all." Some say this was the Tazetta or bunch-flowered narcissus, which man has known the longest.

One Greek myth relates that Europa was in a meadow gathering narcissi when Jupiter, king of the gods, appeared in the field in the shape of a bull. Toward the end of the fifth century, Sophocles wrote of the goddesses on Mt. Olympus, wearing crowns of these flowers.

The story of Persephone, or Proserpina, is also associated with the blossoms. It is said that she was tempted away from her companions by a new flower that Jupiter had created to help his brother Pluto in his plan to carry her to his kingdom in the underworld. While she was gathering the lovely blooms, the earth suddenly opened; a chariot drawn by coal-black horses "dashed out and swept her away." Some say her senses had been dulled by the scent and she had become drowsy. Then the narcissi, in the field where she had been gathering them, formed cups of their petals and caught Persephone's tears in them.

The writer Ovid is reported to have fabricated the often told legend associated with the handsome youth, Narcissus, son of the river goddess. Although he had won the love of the maiden Echo, he did not return it; for he was untouched by this emotion. Because of her unrequited love, Echo pined away, and became just a voice, which could be heard in waste places.

Then Nemesis punished the youth by making him fall in love with his own image, which was reflected in a pool of water. He became so enthralled by it that he could not eat, but just stayed there and admired his own reflection, finally dying of sheer weakness. Or, as some one has suggested, he may have fallen into the water and drowned. The story goes that when the water nymphs came to take his body away, they found white narcissi there. Another version of the myth is that Narcissus killed himself in his grief, and the Poet's Narcissus sprang from his blood.

Alternate December Plant—Holly

> Glad Christmas comes and every hearth
> Makes room to give him welcome now.
> E'en want will dry its tears in mirth
> And crown him with a holly wreath.

For centuries holly, with its traditional colors of red and green, has been symbolic of Christmas; and this attractive plant with smooth, glossy green leaves and gay red berries is a great favorite during the holiday festivities.

Even though its name is believed by many to be a corruption of the word "holy," the use of holly for decorative purposes really comes down to us from early pagan customs. Over 500 years before the birth of the Christ Child, the Romans were gaily celebrating their midwinter feast—the Saturnalia. At that time they would adorn their homes and temples with greenery, including holly. It was customary, too, at this season to send branches of holly, along with gifts, to their friends. To the Romans, holly was an emblem of friendliness and good will.

The ancient peoples of Northern Europe used to hang holly at their doors to shelter the woodland spirits from the chilly winds, and so insure good luck to their homes. Then, when the birds had eaten the berries, these Teutons thought the spirits had gone safely back to their homes.

When these ancient tribes accepted Christianity, they continued to use the plant as decoration during their winter solstice festival— now the anniversary of Christ's birth at Bethlehem. The writer of an English book of the 16th century asserted: "Everyman's house, parish church, and market places were decorated with holly at Christmas."

Alfred Lord Tennyson, the British poet, also described this custom:

> Once again at Christmas did we weave
> The holly round the Christmas hearth;
> The silent snow possessed the earth,
> And calmly fell our Christmas Eve.

With the widespread use of holly at the Yuletide, several customs and legends arose in connection with the plant. In England it was considered bad luck to carry this type of greenery into the house before Christmas Eve, for fear it would provoke family quarrels. Also, persons who had been enemies often used this season to meet under a holly tree and to try to adjust their differences. There was a belief, too, that all holiday greenery must be taken down at Twelfth Night so that no bad luck would come to the home and family.

Nowadays holly is especially popular in England, Canada, and the

United States; where a favorite front door ornament is a large wreath of glistening holly, topped with a red satin ribbon bow. So through the years this bit of greenery has truly caught the Christmas spirit. As one person has feelingly expressed it:

Beautiful, cheery holly, with its glossy, prickly leaves and its coral bells, was a sacred plant in the childhood of the world, and will continue to be a sacred plant as long as the world lasts.

Holly belongs to a large family of trees and shrubs, not all of which are evergreens. Sometimes it is a tall tree—perhaps 40 to 50 feet high; at other times it may be a low shrub, growing decoratively in gardens, or making useful hedges.

Holly grows almost everywhere, both in the temperate and in tropical regions, but not in extremely cold places. More than one hundred varieties are native to Central and South America; others are found in Madagascar, the East Indies, and Asia (especially in China and Japan), however, not so many varieties are found in Europe, Africa, and Australia.

The ordinary English holly is an evergreen shrub, or low tree, with smooth leaves 2 to 3 inches long—(glossier and more ornamental than the variety cultivated in the United States as a garden shrub.) Holly is grown in all of Great Britain (except Northeast Scotland), and in Western and Northern Europe. In England, it is usually small because the larger trees are used for wood. It is rarely hurt by frost in the British Isles, where its foliage and berries make it a valuable ornamental tree. This plant also grows abundantly in France, except for Brittany.

In the United States there are at least a dozen native kinds of holly which grow mainly in the southeastern part of the country. The plant is found along the Atlantic Coast from Massachusetts to Florida, and in the South as far west as Texas; then it is spread northward to the Mississippi Valley, to Missouri and Indiana.

American holly is similar to the British, but the leaves are not so attractive, being rather dull. It grows slowly, but does at times become a tree with a good-sized trunk. Several varieties of holly are grown in the Northwestern states (especially around Puget Sound), and in British Columbia. In these regions it is gathered in large quantities and sold commercially.

The marketing of this greenery at the holiday season is done on a big scale; the most popular type being the English holly, although the native American type also has a wide sale. An unusual Christmas decoration is the so-called "white holly," which is not in fact holly at all, but its leaves do resemble those of this plant. In recent years much of it has been sold in florists' shops in cities because the distinctive appearance of this "desert holly" lends itself to unusual Christmas arrangements.

Besides its role in the holiday decor, holly has been used in other ways. The wood, both of the British and American varieties, is fine-textured, white, and quite hard; often it has been utilized for cabinet work, in turning, and inlaying. Since it takes a black stain well, it is sometimes substituted for ebony, especially for teapot handles. Holly leaves have served as food for deer and sheep, and in some parts of France as winter fodder. Leaves of a South American variety are used to make a native drink, called "maté" (tea).

Holly too, has its legends and superstitions: it is said that witches hated the plant, so some persons grew it around their homes to keep them away. It was also supposed to repel lightning. And people used to concoct a syrup from the bark of the plant as a sure remedy for coughs.

Christ's crown of thorns was believed to have been made from holly, which at that time had white berries, instead of the red ones we know today. But after its use in His crown, the berries turned red as blood. Hence, the holly wreath was used at Christmas as a symbol of His suffering. There were also beliefs that holly sprang up in Christ's footsteps; that animals revered the plant; and that it was from a holly bush in the wilderness that God spoke to Moses.

The well-known English novelist, Emily Brontë, wrote these comparative lines about holly:

> Love is like the wildrose briar;
> Friendship is like the holly tree.
> The holly is dark when the rose-briar blooms,
> But which will bloom most constantly?

Bibliography

Books

ACHELIS, ELIZABETH. *Of Time and the Calendar*. New York: Hermitage House, 1955.

ANDERSON, A. W. *Coming of the Flowers*. New York: Farrar, Straus and Young, 1959.

ASIMOV, ISAAC. *The Clock We Live On*. New York: Abelard-Schuman, 1959.

BARTLETT, JOHN. *Familiar Quotations*. London: Macmillan Company, 1957.

BLANCHARD, NELTJE. *Nature's Garden*. New York: Doubleday Page Company, 1904.

CAREY, N. C. *Flower Legends*. London: Pearson, 1921.

CLEMENTS, EDITH S. *Flowers of Coast and Sierra*. New York: W. W. Wilson Company, 1928.

COATS, ALICE M. *Flowers and Their Histories*. New York: Pitman Publishing Company, 1956.

FISCHER, HELEN P. *The Flower Family Album*. St. Louis: J. S. Swift Company, 1940.

FOLEY, D. J. *Flowers for Your Garden*. New York: Macmillan Company, 1938.

GOLENPAUL, DAN, ASSOCIATES. *Information Please Almanac and Year Book*. New York: McGraw-Hill Company, 1961.

HAUSMAN, ETHEL H. *Illustrated Encyclopedia of American Wild Flowers*. Garden City, N.Y.: Garden City Publishing Company, 1947.

HELLYER, A. G. L. *Flowers in Color*. London: W. H. and L. Collingridge, 1955.

HOLLINGSWORTH, BUCKNER. *Flower Chronicles*. New Brunswick, N.J.: Rutgers University Press, 1958.

HONE, WILLIAM. *Everyday Book*. London: William Tegg, 1864.

———. *Table Book*. London: William Tegg, 1864.

————. *Year Book of Daily Recreation and Information.* London: William Tegg, 1864.

HOTTES, A. C. *Book of Annuals.* New York: A. T. De La Mare Company, 1942.

HOUSE, HOMER D. *Wild Flowers.* New York: Macmillan Company, 1935.

HOWE, BEA. *Lady with Green Fingers.* London: Country Life Ltd., 1961.

JENKINS, DOROTHY N. *Annual Flowers.* New York: M. Barrows and Company, 1945.

KEELER, L. HARRIET. *Our Garden Flowers.* New York: Charles Scribner's Sons, 1910.

KRAUS, EDWARD H. *Gems and Gem Materials.* New York: McGraw-Hill, 1947.

KRYTHE, MAYMIE R. *All About American Holidays.* New York: Harper & Row, 1962.

————. *All About Christmas.* New York: Harper & Row, 1954.

LEYMARIE, JEAN. *Impressionism.* Paris: Syndicat de la Propriete.

LIDDICOAT, R. T., JR. *Handbook of Gem Identification.* Los Angeles: Gemological Institute of America, 1947.

LINTON, RALPH AND ADELIN. *Lore of Birthdays.* New York: Henry Schuman, Inc., 1952.

MANTEGAGAZZA, PAOLO. *Legends of Flowers.* (translated by Mrs. Alexander Kennedy), New York: A. Garfish.

McCURDY, R. M. *Book of Garden Flowers.* Garden City, New York: Doubleday Page and Company, 1926.

McDONALD, LUCILE S. *Jewels and Gems.* New York: T. Y. Crowell, 1940.

MYERS, WILLIAM M. AND ANDERSON, C. O. *Garnet: Its Mining, Milling and Utilization.* Washington, D.C.: Department of Commerce, Bureau of Mines, Bulletin 256, 1925.

PEARLY, RICHARD M. *Popular Gemology.* Denver, Colorado: Sage Books, 1948.

PRATT, GLADYS L. *American Garden Flowers.* New York: Random House, 1943.

QUINN, VERNON. *Stories and Legends of Garden Flowers.* New York: F. A. Stokes Company, 1939.

ROSS, ISHBEL. *Charmers and Cranks.* New York: Harper and Row, 1965.

SEITZ, WILLIAM C. *Claude Monet: Seasons and Moments.* Garden City, N.Y.: Doubleday, 1960.

SINGLETON, ESTHER. *The Shakespeare Garden.* New York: Century Company, 1922.

SKINNER, M. C. *Myths and Legends of Flowers, Trees, Fruits, and Plants.* Philadelphia: J. B. Lippincott, 1940.

SMITH, G. F. *Gemstones.* New York: Pitman Publishing Company, 1958.

SPENCER, L. J. *A Key to Precious Stones.* London and Glasgow: Blackie and Son, Ltd., 1936.

SWENGEL, HOPE L. *The Romance of Your Birthstone*. New York: American Museum of Natural History, 1928.
TAILLANDER, YVON. *Monet*. New York: Crown Publishing Co.
TAYLOR, NORMAN. *The Everblooming Garden*. Toronto, New York, London: D. Van Nostrand Company, Inc., 1953.
————. *The Guide to Garden Flowers*. Boston: Houghton Mifflin Company, 1959.
WEBSTER, ROBERT F. *Practical Gemology*. London: N.A.G. Press, Ltd., 1952.
WEINSTEIN, MICHAEL. *Precious and Semi-Precious Stones*. London: Sir Isaac Pitman & Sons, Ltd., 1946.
WHITLOCK, HERBERT P. *The Story of the Gems*. New York: Emerson Books, Inc., 1946.
WILKINS, JAMES H., Editor. *The Great Diamond Hoax and Other Stirring Incidents in the Life of Asbury Harpending*. Norman, Oklahoma: University of Oklahoma Press, 1959.
WILSON, ALBERT. *How Does Your Garden Grow?* Menlo Park, California: Happy Hours, 1949.
WILSON, P. W. *Romance of the Calendar*. New York: W. W. Norton Company, Inc., 1937.

ENCYCLOPEDIAS

American People's Encyclopedia. Chicago: Spencer Press, Inc., 1949–1961.
Collier's Encyclopedia. New York, Toronto: P. F. Collier and Son Corporation, 1959.
Compton's Pictured Encyclopedia. Chicago: F. E. Compton Company, 1910.
Dictionary of National Biography. (Edited by Stephens, Leslie and Lee, Sidney), London: Macmillan Company, 1908.
Encyclopedia Americana. New York: American Corporation, 1959.
Encyclopaedia Britannica. London, Toronto: 1960.
Funk and Wagnall's Standard Reference Encyclopedia. (J. L. Mores, Editor-in-Chief), New York: Standard Reference Works Publishing Company, Inc., 1959.
National Encyclopedia of American Biography. New York: James T. White and Company, 1927, 1946.
New International Encyclopedia. New York: Dodd, Mead and Company, 1915.
Picture World Encyclopedia. New York: Picture World Encyclopedia, Inc., 1959.
Twentieth Century Dictionary. (Edited by Geddie, William, and Chambers, R.), London: George Newnes, Ltd., 1959.
World Book Encyclopedia. Chicago: Field Enterprises, Inc., 1965.

MAGAZINE ARTICLES

ATKINSON, DR. R. E., "Four Great New Roses," *Los Angeles Times Home Magazine*, May 21, 1961.

BAIRD, RUTH E., "Mother's Day Flower," *Southland Magazine*, May 13, 1951.

BENGSTON, BENNIE, "Story of the Calendar," *Classmate*, January 19, 1951.

BEVIS, KATHERINE, "Story of the Calendar," *Conquest*, January, 1953.

COLEMAN, CAROLINE, "Newest Early Birds," *Southland Magazine*, January 13, 1966.

DE MANCHE, DON, "New Rose Joins Royalty," *Southland Magazine*, May 21, 1961.

EMERY, ELISE, "Embarking on a Diamond Expedition?," *Long Beach Press-Telegram*, April 23, 1961.

EWERS, RETTA E., "Lost Emeralds of the Santa Rosas," *Southland Magazine*, October 10, 1963.

FAULKNER, J. P., "America's Only Diamond Mine," *Coronet*, 1956.

FORD, MIRIAM ALLEN, "Asbury Harpending, Boy Wonder," *Ghost Town News*, October, 1942.

GILMORE, BOB, "Carnations for Fragrance," *Southland Magazine*, February, 1952.

GOLDIN, H. L., "1963's Rose Queens," *Southland Magazine*, May 6, 1962.

———, "New Royalty of Regal Roses," *Southland Magazine*, June 16, 1963.

GOTTLIEB, EDWARD, "Daffodils: the Poet's Choice," *Southland Magazine*, January 2, 1966.

HURLEY, MARTHA, "How Fair Is the Rose," *Southland Magazine*.

KEMMERER, J. B., "The Pearl Harvest from the Sea," *Southland Magazine*, January 31, 1960.

KERIGAN, FLORENCE, "Precious Cargo," *Classmate*, August 4, 1957.

LASCH, GEORGE, "New Glads Make Debut," *Southland Magazine*, December 18, 1960.

LATHAM, SID, "The Quest for Fiery Opals," *True Magazine*, January, 1966.

LECHLER, RENÉ, "Queen Elizabeth, Is She the Richest Woman in the World?" *Parade*, December 26, 1965.

MASKEY, CARL, "Bulbs Planted in the Spring Produce Color in the Spring."

MCHENDRIE, JANET, "Romance of the Rose," *Los Angeles Times Home Magazine*.

MCLEOD, A. C., "New in Marigolds," *Southland Magazine*, January 2, 1966.

MILLER, WILLIAM C., "The Illicit Poppy Fruit," *Southland Magazine*, October 10, 1965.

MORTON, RACHEL, "Major and Minor Notes," *Long Beach Press-Telegram*, January 27, 1962.

PAULEY, GAY, "History Walks Along the Gem-Encrusted Path," *Long Beach Press-Telegram*, December 29, 1961.

SHEPPARD, EUGENIA, "Emeralds Outrank Diamonds as Glamour Stones," *Gazette*, Montreal, Canada, October 1, 1965.

SHIPP, CAMERON, "Miracle of the Diamond," *Coronet*, 1946.

TOOKER, DOROTHY, "January Birthstones," *Classmate*, January 23, 1949.

——, "Jonquils for March," *Classmate*, February 26, 1953.

——, "June Birthstones," *Classmate*, June 26, 1949.

——, "Lily of the Valley for May," *Classmate*, May 28, 1950.

——, "March Birthstones," *Classmate*, March 27, 1949.

——, "May Birthstones," *Classmate*, May, 1949.

WALGREN, MRS. MYRTLE, "Flowers for Your Garden," *Together*, April, 1964.

YATES, VIRGINIA, " 'If You Dig Daisies,' This Is Your Show," *Los Angeles Times*, January 11, 1966.

ZINZER, BEN, "Morning Glory Seeds Give Hallucinations," *Long Beach Press-Telegram*, July 10, 1964.

——, "The Fire of Diamonds," *Los Angeles Times Home Magazine*, May, 1949.

——, "The New Roses," *Los Angeles Times Home Magazine*, January 8, 1961.

——, "Two Opulent New Marigolds," *Los Angeles Times Home Magazine*, February 7, 1961.

PAMPHLETS

CHASE, H. V. AND W. D., *Chase's Calendar of Annual Events*, Flint, Michigan: Appletree Press, 1965.

THOMAS, ROBERT B., *The Old Farmer's Almanac*, Dublin, New Hampshire: Yankee, Inc., 1960.

——, *Introduction to Brazilian Gem Stones*, Rio de Janiero, Brazil: H. Stern Company.

Index

precious stones to the fabulous 44.5 carat "Hope" diamond; and flowers, from the common little field daisy to the most resplendent rose. Their origins and their often bewitching roles in history are all here.

Important events that have taken place in each century and in every country are related here. Famous statesmen, royalty, dignitaries, actors, sports figures, and other personalities whose birthdays fall in a given month are mentioned. ALL ABOUT THE MONTHS is a storehouse of information that makes fascinating reading for everyone, and will surely prove a boon to those who plan programs built around the months of the year.

ALL ABOUT THE AUTHOR

MAYMIE R. KRYTHE, who was born in Springfield, Ohio, has lived in five western states and traveled in all the others except Alaska. She received her A.B. from Wittenberg University and her A.M. in English from the University of Southern California. She has also studied at the University of Jena and University of Berlin, in Germany. Since 1923 she has lived in Long Beach, California where for some years she taught English and German.

Mrs. Krythe has lectured on early California history, Christmas traditions, and her many travels. She has taken three trips around the world, each of six months' duration, visiting Australia, Suez, Europe, South America, South Africa, Indonesia, and other parts of the Orient. On ten other occasions she toured Europe.